The Netherlands in a Nutshell

The Netherlands in a Nutshell

HIGHLIGHTS FROM DUTCH HISTORY AND CULTURE

AMSTERDAM UNIVERSITY PRESS

entoen·nu

www.entoen.nu

© 2008 Frits van Oostrom | Stichting entoen.nu

ISBN 978-90-8964-039-0
NUR 688/840

Published by Amsterdam University Press, the Netherlands
www.aup.nl

Design: Kok Korpershoek, Amsterdam, the Netherlands

Contents

When we, as individuals, pick and mix cultural elements for ourselves, we do not do so indiscriminately, but according to our natures. Societies, too, must retain the ability to discriminate, to reject as well as to accept, to value some things above others, and to insist on the acceptance of those values by all their members. [...] If we are to build a plural society on the foundation of what unites us, we must face up to what divides. But the questions of core freedoms and primary loyalties can't be ducked. No society, no matter how tolerant, can expect to thrive if its citizens don't prize what their citizenship means – if, when asked what they stand for as Frenchmen, as Indians, as Britons, they cannot give clear replies.

SALMAN RUSHDIE[1]

Some etymologists speculate that the word 'canon' (as in 'canonical') is related to the Arabic word *qanum*, or law in the binding, legalistic sense of the word. But that is only one rather restrictive meaning. The other is a musical one, canon as a contrapuntal form employing numerous voices in usually strict imitation of each other, a form, in other words, expressing motion, playfulness, discovery, and, in the rhetorical sense, invention. Viewed this way, the canonical humanities, far from being a rigid tablet of fixed rules and monuments bullying us from the past [...] will always remain open to changing combination of sense and signification.

EDWARD SAID[2]

6

1   Rushdie 2005.
2   Said 2004, p. 25.

Foreword

What basic knowledge of Dutch history and culture should we pass on to
future generations of Dutch citizens? This was the difficult question facing the
Committee for the Development of the Dutch Canon in 2005, when the Minister of
Education, Culture and Science asked it to design a canon of the Netherlands.

The result is a canon in fifty key topics, or 'windows': important people, inventions
and events which together show how the Netherlands has developed into the
country that it now is. Each Dutch student will become familiar with these
windows at school. In this book, the fifty windows sit together as the Netherlands
in a nutshell, to anyone who would like to make a quick acquaintance with this
low country by the sea.

Each window includes a list of places to visit and websites. At the back of the book,
there is an overview of the fifty windows, grouped in fourteen 'main lines'.

It has become a truly Dutch canon because it was created in a typically Dutch way:
it was not decreed by a central authority or a single lofty institution, and neither
was it created by a majority vote in a referendum.

This canon was created by bringing together a number of specialists and allowing
them to consult for a year with one another and with a selection of interested
individuals and stakeholders. A website that featured a discussion forum gave every
Dutch citizen the opportunity to voice his or her opinion. The process brings to
mind the way in which the Netherlands has succeeded for centuries in keeping
its polders dry: collective craftsmanship.

The way in which this canon was created says as much about the Netherlands
as do the fifty windows themselves.

The canon of the Netherlands

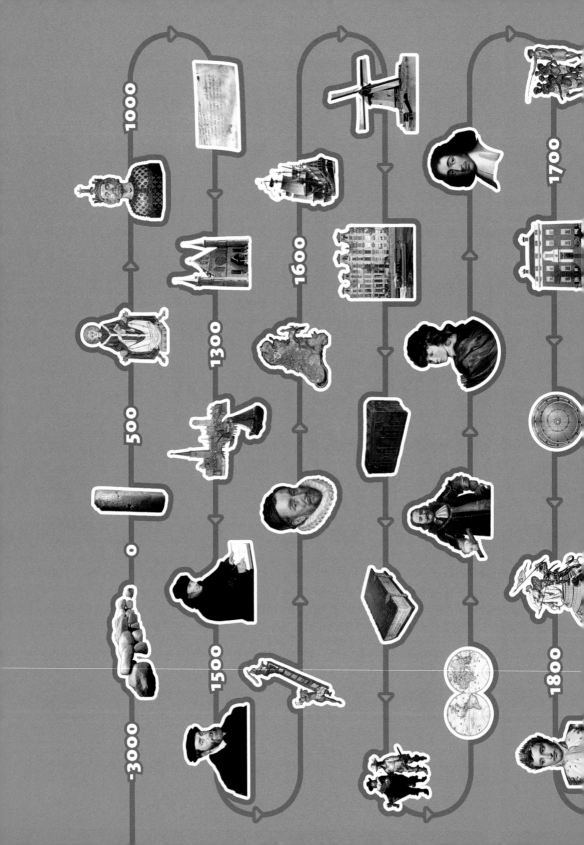

1000

1700

1600

1300

500

0

-3000

1500

1800

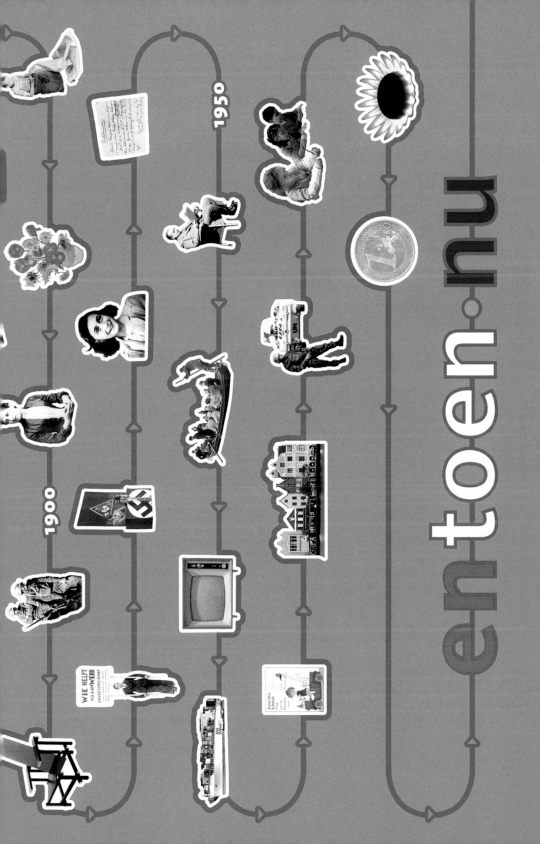

1950

1900

en · toen · nu

Megalithic tombs
Early farmers

People were already living in the Low Countries when the world was five thousand years younger than it is today. What little they left behind is usually buried deep in the ground. However, in the province of Drenthe, you can see traces of them above the ground. Their megaliths: giant stones that people set in formations and piled up on one another. They were used as tombs. This type of chamber tomb was relatively common at the time, but certainly not all such tombs were built with enormous erratic blocks. These huge boulders were only to be found in Drenthe, Denmark and northern Germany and must have been transported there by glaciers during one of the ice ages some 150,000 years ago.

Archaeological excavations in and around megalithic tombs have not uncovered any skeletons – bones have completely disintegrated after so many thousands of

years – but funerary gifts placed with the deceased for use in the afterlife have been found. These gifts include pots known as "funnel beakers" due to their shape. Based on these and other finds, archaeologists have constructed a picture of the way of life of these first generations of farmers. They were the first people in the region to leave behind their hunter-gatherer existence and settle in a fixed place. They lived in wattle and daub farmhouses, used wooden and stone tools and made pots for storage. Undoubtedly they also made agreements regarding ownership and the administration of justice, but we can no longer discover what these were because these early farmers had no written language. Their society had no written records.

How these people were able to raise stones from the ground that sometimes weighed 20,000 kilos, without any machinery, is still not completely clear. Perhaps they built earthen ramps and used small logs to roll the stones. Once the stones were in place, the ground underneath them could have been dug away to create a chamber tomb.

In Drenthe, over fifty megalithic tombs have remained preserved. There must have been many more at one time, because over the centuries a great many megaliths have disappeared, for instance, because the stones were used for building.

References

Places to Go
Alphen aan den Rijn: Archeon
Assen: Drents Museum (Girl of Yde)
Borger: Hunebedcentrum Borger (Hunebed Centre)
Delfzijl: Muzeeaquarium (Iron Age findings)
Dongen: IJzertijdboerderij (reconstruction of a farm dating
    from the Iron Age)

Websites
www.archeon.nl
www.britannica.com/EBchecked/topic/276562/hunebed
www.drentsmuseum.nl
www.hunebedcentrum.nl
www.minbuza.nl/history/en/ontstaan,Before-50-BC.html

Captions
[page 12] *Megalithic tomb*, ANP/Koen Suyk
[above] *Megalithic tomb of Loon*, archives of
    Leendert P. Louwe Kooymans
[left] *Funnel beaker*, Rijksmuseum van Oudheiden

47 AD - circa 400 AD
The Roman Limes
On the frontiers of the Roman world

Two thousand years ago, one of the frontiers of the immense Roman Empire ran through the Low Countries. The River Rhine that flowed from Nijmegen via Utrecht and Alphen aan den Rijn to the sea at Katwijk, formed part of the Roman *Limes*, the Latin word for frontier. In the eyes of the Romans, the uncivilised world began north of the river. That was where Germanic and Celtic tribes lived, including the Frisians and the Canninefates. The Rhine was, however, not just a frontier. It was also a major transport channel for the Romans. Supplies were brought in and exported by ship.

The Romans built watchtowers and army camps at regular intervals along the Rhine to defend their territory against enemy attacks from the north. Most of the encampments could house several hundred soldiers, but close to Nijmegen a camp arose that could accommodate two legions of six thousand men. The presence of these well-trained soldiers in their tunics, with their shiny

helmets, shields and swords, must have made quite an impression on the local population. Moreover, the surrounding areas changed dramatically with the introduction of Roman architecture.

South of the frontier – in Roman territory – lived, among others, the Batavians. They lived in peace with the Romans and many Batavians served in the Roman army. However, in 69 A.D. they rose up against the Romans, profiting from the unrest that had broken out across the entire Roman Empire following the death of the Emperor Nero. The Batavians were led by Julius Civilis, a Batavian who had already served twenty-five years in the Roman army. For a short time it seemed as if the rebellion would be successful, but after a few months the Romans defeated the Batavians. Julius Civilis had achieved nothing. Nonetheless, he was honoured as a true hero centuries later. Sixteenth century scholars claimed that the Batavians had rebelled for love of freedom and that they should therefore be regarded as the true forefathers of the Dutch. This says more about the scholars than it does about the Batavians.

In the fourth century AD, more and more Germanic tribes invaded Roman territory. As a result, the Romans ultimately withdrew to behind the Alps.

Various places along the Rhine in the Netherlands have their origins in Roman times, as you can see on a medieval copy of an ancient Roman map. Finds are still being made at new archaeological excavations. For example, a watchtower and two ships were unearthed when the new Leidsche Rijn district was being built near Utrecht.

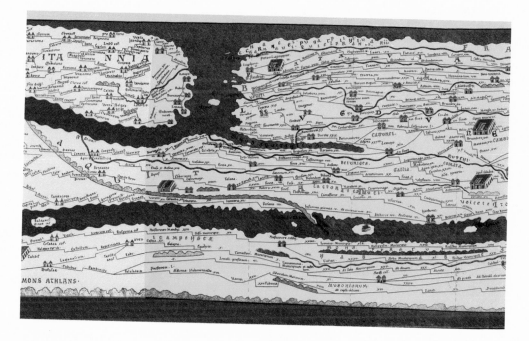

References

Places to Go

Alphen aan den Rijn: Archeon
Assen: Drents Museum
Heerlen: Thermenmuseum
Leiden: Rijksmuseum van Oudheden
    (National Museum of Antiquities)
Lelystad: Bataviawerf (excavated Roman ship)
Nijmegen: Museum het Valkhof
The Hague: Museon (four Roman 'limes' found
    in The Hague)
Xanten (Germany): 'Römerroute' (bicycle route)
Venlo: Limburgs Museum (Romans in Limburg)
Woerden: Stadsmuseum Woerden (findings from
    a Roman military camp)

Websites

www.archeon.nl
www.bataviawerf.nl
www.belvedere.nu
www.britannica.com/EBchecked/topic/55763/Batavia
www.castellumhogewoerd.nl
www.minbuza.nl/history/en/ontstaan,50-v--Chr---400.html
www.museumhetvalkhof.nl
www.rmo.nl
www.xanten.de/nl/toerisme/thema_routes/roemerroute

Captions

[page 14] *Milestone*, Archeologische Dienst, The Hague
[above] *Tabula Peutingeriana, Conradi Milleri*,
    Bibliotheca Augustana

658 AD - 739 AD

Willibrord

The spread of Christianity

In 690 AD, Willibrord, an English monk from Northumbria, landed at the then mouth of the Rhine where the town of Katwijk is now situated. Together with a group of colleagues he wished to spread Christianity throughout the land of the Frisians. The Frisians lived in the coastal region stretching from the Westerschelde to near Dokkum. Their territory bordered on that of the Frankish kings, who had converted to the Christian faith a century earlier. The port town of Dorestad aan de Rijn and the settlement of Utrecht were situated on the border. This was not a permanent border, because battles regularly broke out and the border would shift as the Frisians moved slightly to the south or the Franks to the north. During a period of success, in 630 AD a Frankish king had built the first church in Utrecht at the place where the Dom now stands. Shortly afterwards, however, the church had been destroyed by the Frisians.

Willibrord's predecessors had experienced that converting the heathen Frisians would be no easy task. For this reason, Willibrord first sought support. He paid several visits to the Frankish king and the Pope in Rome. The latter appointed Willbrord Archbishop of the Frisians. In 696 AD, Willibrord settled in Utrecht. He rebuilt the church destroyed earlier by the Frisians and commissioned the building of a new church dedicated to San Salvator, or, in other words, Jesus Christ.

Subsequently, missionaries left Utrecht for the lands of the Frisians. They were successful and by the end of Willibrord's life – he died in 739 AD – the new faith had the upper hand in the coastal region. In the rest of Frisian territory, however, resistance to the new faith was strong. The local nobility regarded the missionaries as accomplices of the Franks and they clung to the old ways and their gods like Wodan and Donar. It was only at the end of the eighth century AD that Frankish weapons finally crushed the Frisian resistance.

References

Places to Go

Dokkum: Bonifatius Chapel, Bonifatius Spring, art work 'Martelaarsveld'
Echternach (Luxemburg): Abby of Echternach (founded by Willibrord, grave of Willibrord)
Utrecht: Museum Catharijneconvent
Utrecht: Kerkenkruis (five churches together form a Christian cross)

Websites

www.britannica.com/EBchecked/topic/644473/ Saint-Willibrord
www.catharijneconvent.nl
www.dongeradeel.nl
www.fordham.edu/halsall/basis/alcuin-willbrord.html

Captions

[page 16] *Willibrord*, Bibliothèque Nationale de France/ Latin 10510
[above] *Digital visualisation of the Chapel of the Holy Cross and the St. Servator church,* DeroDe3D/Rijntjes/Stöver

742 AD - 814 AD

Charlemagne
Emperor of the Land of the Setting Sun

Charlemagne was the most important king of the early Middle Ages. In 771 AD he became King of the Franks, whose territory included what would be the Low Countries. Charlemagne was at war throughout his entire reign: against the Moslem rulers of the Iberian peninsula, against the Langobards in the south and against the Saxons and the Danes in north-western Europe. Charlemagne was successful because he managed to expand the kingdom of the Franks into an empire that encompassed large parts of what we know today as Europe. On Christmas day 800 AD, the Pope crowned Charlemagne Emperor of the West.

To govern his enormous empire, Charlemagne used "vassals" or liegemen who had to serve him "in word and deed". They had to advise him on all kinds of administrative matters and serve him as

warriors in times of war. In exchange, they received a "fief" from Charlemagne, control over and the revenues of a large area of land. The vassals in turn often divided their land among tenants. Initially, the agreements terminated on the death of the vassal, but over the course of time the vassals began to regard their fiefs as hereditary possessions and adopted an increasingly independent position in respect of their liege lord.

Charlemagne kept palaces throughout his empire. Such a palace was known as a "palts". Charlemagne travelled from palts to palts arranging his affairs with his vassals on the spot. He also had a palts in Nijmegen: the Valkhof. Here, Charlemagne busied himself, among other things, with the situation in the Frisian bishopric and kept abreast of the campaign of his armies against the heathen Saxons. Charlemagne's first biographer, the monk Einhard, regarded this 33-year-long battle as the "longest, most horrible, and, for the Frankish people, the most exacting war he ever waged".

Charlemagne set great store by education, culture and science. Although he himself could barely write his own name, he was accomplished in maths and astronomy and he spoke several languages. Charlemagne established schools to train young noblemen for serving the empire. He also was in contact with the Moslem world through the Caliph of Baghdad, Harun al-Rashid, who gave him an elephant as a gift.

In the last years of his life, Charlemagne settled down in his palace complex at Aix-en-Chapelle, where he was buried in 814 AD. His palace chapel formed the basis for the present Cathedral (the Dom), where his throne and elaborately-decorated coffin can still be seen today.

Even in his own lifetime, many stories went around about Charlemagne. After his death they became even more expansive and embellished; people started to regard him as a saint. Charlemagne is considered one of the greatest kings in history.

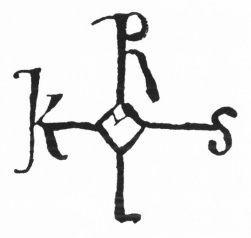

References

Places to Go
Aachen (Germany): Cathedral, treasury
Nijmegen: The Valkhof (park)

Websites
www.aachen.de
www.britannica.com/EBchecked/topic/106546/
    Charlemagne
www.fordham.edu/halsall/basis/einhard.html
www.minbuza.nl/history/en/ontstaan,800.html
www.museumhetvalkhof.nl

Captions
[page 18] *Bust of Charlemagne*, Domkapitel Aachen/
    Ann Münchow
[above] *Signature of Charlemagne*
[left] *Portrait of Charlemagne*, Albrecht Dürer,
    Germanisches Nationalmuseum, Nuremberg

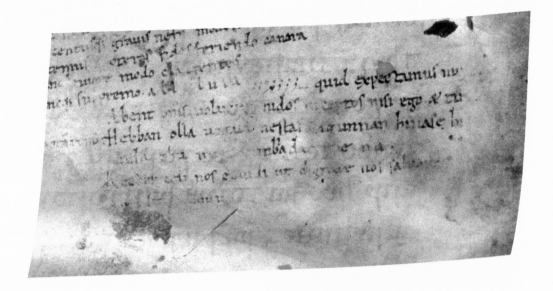

circa 1100
Hebban olla vogala
The Dutch language in writing

Hebban olla vogala nestas hagunnan hinase
hic anda thu, wat unbidan we nu?

The above is a Dutch sentence, although at
first sight it's barely recognisable as such.
This is because it is about the earliest
piece of written Dutch we have, some one
thousand years old. It literally says: Have all
birds nests started except me and you;
what wait we for, or: All birds have started
making nests, except you and me, what are
we waiting for? These lines are probably
from a love song, the oldest Dutch love song
you could say.

These lines were written to test a quill
pen in about 1100 by a Flemish monk
who was staying in an English monastery. His
daily life was largely filled with copying
Latin and Old English texts. Now and then
he had to sharpen the goose quill he used

for writing. On the last page of the book
he was copying he would try out his newly
sharpened pen before continuing his
copying. In such instances he wrote the
first thing that came into his head. For this
monk, it was a love poem that he remembered
from his youth in Flanders: *Hebban olla*
vogala...

This was simply an incident that only
with the wisdom of many centuries could
be regarded as the beginning of a new
phenomenon: the use of the Dutch language
as a medium for written literature. That the
first fruits of the pen in Dutch were written
in a monastery and were preserved in a
sacred monastic book is, of course, no
coincidence. Writing had long been the
domain of monks and the written word was
mainly used for the sacred, Latin texts of
the church.

21

References

Places to Go

Ter Apel: Klooster Ter Apel (monastery with reconstructed scriptorium, in which manuscripts and books are exhibited)

The Hague: Museum Meermanno (museum about (the history) of the handwritten and printed book; in the scriptorium one can try to write with a goose feather)

Zuthphen: Librije (medieval library of St. Walburg's Church)

Websites

www.kb.nl/manuscripts
www.meermanno.nl

Captions

[page 20] *Latin handwriting from the abbey of Rochester*, Bodleian Library, Oxford/MS. Bodl. 340, fol. 169v.

[left] *Parchment seller*, Hs. Kopenhagen, Kongelige Bibliotek, GKS F4, bd. 1, f. 183r.

[right] *Scriptorium initial from the Rooklooster with writing monk*, Hs. Brussel, Koninklijke Bibliotheek, 213, fol. 2r.

1254 - 1296
Floris V
A Dutch count and disgruntled nobles

Today, the "Binnenhof" is symbolic of the Dutch political scene that has its home in The Hague. Few people realise that the history of the complex goes back to the thirteenth century and is closely linked to the period in which the most famous medieval Count of Holland, Floris V, ruled. When Floris was born in the summer of 1254, a new castle was being built in *des Graven Haghe* (The Hague). Floris's father, Count William II had commissioned the building. In 1256, during an expedition against the Frisians near Hoogwoud, Count William and his horse fell through the ice. The Frisians were quick to rush up and smash in his skull. At only two years old, Floris was now officially the new count, although power was temporarily vested in the hands of his uncle.

Once he gained his majority, Floris decided to avenge his father's death by conquering the Frisians. The campaign was a huge failure and allowed the peasants

and town-dwellers in Kennemerland the opportunity to rebel. Floris was only able to quell the rebellion by granting Kennemerland a number of privileges that would afford the inhabitants protection from the noble lords. The indignant nobles sneeringly called Floris: "Der keerlen god", the god of the peasants.

In the years that followed, however, Floris was able to expand the territory of the counts of Holland considerably: he snatched the Amstel region and Woerden from the Bishop of Utrecht (thereby making the very young Amsterdam a town of Holland) and he conquered West Friesland. To consolidate his victories, Floris had citadels built near Alkmaar, Medemblik and Wijdenes.

In about 1280, the new castle in The Hague was finally completed with its proud Great Hall (literally the Knight's Hall, *Ridderzaal*), symbol of chivalry, regal and imposing in style as Floris had desired. Floris had a second castle built: Muider Castle (Muiderslot).

In 1296, Floris' rebellious vassals Gijsbrecht van Amstel, Gerard van Velzen and Herman van Woerden took him prisoner in Muider Castle. The peasant population trekked to the castle to demand the release of their count. The three conspirators fled the castle with their prisoner, in the hope of escaping the angry peasant mob. They had tied Floris' legs together under his horse's belly and when he tried to escape he ended up in a ditch where his captors slashed him to death with their swords.

References

Places to Go

Alkmaar: Grote of Sint-Laurenskerk (burial place of partial remains of Floris V)
The Hague: Binnenhof
Muiden: Muiderslot (castle, incl. falconer)
Medemblik: Kasteel Radboud (castle)
Rijnsburg: Museum Oud Rijnsburg (Floris V and the St. Jacob's Order)

Websites

www.binnenhofbezoek.nl
www.britannica.com/EBchecked/topic/210902/Floris-V
www.muiderslot.nl

Captions

[page 22] *Ridderzaal*, ANP/Cees van Leeuwen
[above] *Muiden Castle*, Klaas Lingbeek-Van Kranen
[left] *Engraving of Floris V, Principes Hollandie et Zelandie, Domi Frisiae*, Michiel Vosmeer

1356 - circa 1450

The Hanseatic League

Trading towns in the Low Countries

In the long period from the twelfth to the sixteenth century, the towns of Zutphen, Deventer, Tiel, Kampen, Zwolle and others (particularly in the east of the country) were important and prosperous trading centres. They were members of the Hanseatic League. A Hansa was originally a collaborative arrangement between merchants in various cities who traded in the same goods. By working together they could reduce their costs, travel more safely (together), make purchases or sell in bulk, and arm themselves against the capricious whims of liege lords. In 1356, the Hansa towns formed a league of not just merchants but whole towns. The decision to form the league was made in Lubeck, a town in what is modern-day Germany. The German *Hanze*, which is called the Hanseatic League in English, became a powerful collaborative network of towns that stretched across Germany, the Netherlands, Belgium, the Baltic States, Norway and Poland. Within its network, the league attempted to alleviate restrictions on trade as far as possible. The Hansa network also traded with partners outside this area, with London, for example, and even with Spanish cities.

Trade was brisk in such goods as salt, grains, fish, wood, wine, beer, animal skins and cloth. The goods were mainly transported by sea and on rivers using so-called 'cogs' (ships) of between fifteen to thirty metres in length. The towns grew and prospered, built city walls and became dotted with merchant's homes, warehouses and many other types of buildings. The legacy of the Hanseatic League can still be seen in the towns mentioned above, as well as in smaller Hansa towns like Hasselt and Doesburg.

For non-Hansa towns like Amsterdam, trade across the Baltic Sea was the so-called "mother of all trade". This trade formed the basis for an economic boom. It also meant that this trade centre had to compete with the towns along the IJssel. When the Hanseatic League collapsed in the course of the sixteenth century, the Baltic Sea trade through towns outside the league continued to flourish. By 1585, Antwerp had become the true centre of trade and this position was later taken over by Amsterdam. Shortly afterwards, Dutch trade became increasingly focused on all the seven seas and became embedded in the conquest and exploitation of colonies. The shifting economic relationships in Europe resulted in the towns along the IJssel losing their prominent position.

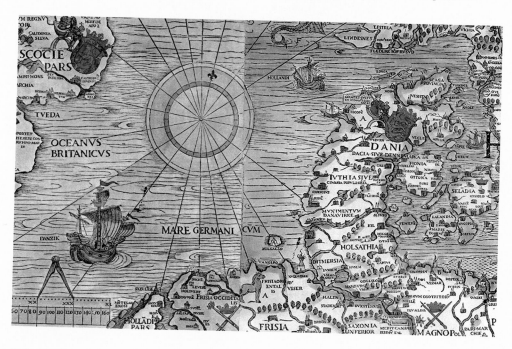

References

Places to Go

Deventer: Historisch Museum Deventer
   (Deventer Historical Museum)
Tourist information office Deventer: 'Hanze-Speurneus',
   a walk through Deventer on the subject of the Hanze
Groningen: Noordelijk Scheepvaartmuseum
   (Northern Maritime Museum)
Kampen: a visit to a reconstructed fourteenth-century
   cog from Kampen
Tourist information office Kampen:
   'Hanzestadswandeling', a walk through Kampen
   on the subject of the Hanze

Websites

www.britannica.com/EBchecked/topic/254543/
   Hanseatic-League
www.deventer.nl/Toerisme/MuseaListing
www.vvvdeventer.nl
www.hanzesteden.info
www.hum.uit.no/a/svenonius/lingua/flow/co/texts/
   hansa.en.html
www.vvvkampen.nl
www.rug.nl/let/onderzoek/onderzoekcentra/
   hanzestudiecentrum/publicaties
   (bibliography on the Hanseatic League)

Captions

[page 24] *View of Zwolle*, Stedelijk Museum Zwolle
[above] *Carta marina of the Baltic Sea, Olaus Magnus*,
   Royal Library, Stockholm

1469? - 1536

Erasmus

An international humanist

Erasmus had a complicated relationship with the land of his birth. He liked to call himself Desiderius Erasmus of Rotterdam, and yet repeatedly criticised the coarse manners and lack of taste of his fellow town-dwellers and country folk.

He was probably born in 1469 as the illegitimate son of a priest. This meant that a future as a monk was the obvious choice. After completing his training at a seminary of the Brethren of the Common Life, among other places, he joined the Augustinian monastery in Steyn near Gouda. Erasmus was taken with the monastery's library and immersed himself in the world of classical antiquity through the writings of classical authors and Italian humanists. The latter, with their enormous learning and critical approach, brought ancient times closer than ever before.

Monastic life with its strict regime and duties was suffocating. Erasmus's extraordinary knowledge of Latin gave him the opportunity to leave the monastery.

He travelled as an independent scholar across large areas of Europe, living from the income from his writing and gifts from a growing multitude of admirers. Erasmus stayed in contact with friends, like-minded scholars and informants through an extensive correspondence network.
In 1500 he wrote *Adagia*, one of the world's first bestsellers, courtesy of the still new printing press. This collection of classical proverbs offered readers a speed course in the lifestyle and way of thinking of the humanists. In addition, Erasmus published books on etiquette, guides for heads of state, and dialogues and tracts that were aimed at educating lords and commoners to be good and responsible Christians.

Erasmus was the first to apply the humanist critical approach to Christian writings. He studied Greek specifically to read the writings of the early founders of the Church and the texts of the New Testament in the original language. This resulted in a series of new critical editions of early Christian writings, including a new edition of the New Testament in Greek with a new translation in Latin. With this *Novum Instrumentum*, Erasmus expressly distanced himself from the Vulgate (the official Church translation) and defended the right to adopt a critical approach to the Bible with the aim of strengthening the perception of faith. Erasmus hoped that one day everyone would be able to quote the Bible – the farmer behind his plough, the weaver at his loom and the traveller on his journey; he believed that even women should read the Bible. His ideal was the attainment of tranquil, austere devotion rooted in inner reflection.

In the polarisation that began in 1517 with the religious reforms of Martin Luther, Erasmus did not want to adopt a position – or did not dare to. He was not prepared to break away from the Catholic Church and hoped that the differences that had arisen could be resolved with sound reasoning. This caused him to be criticised by both sides. Erasmus died in the summer of 1536 at the home of the printer Froben, in Basel.

References

Places to Go

Brussels (Belgium): The Erasmus House
Rotterdam: Huis van Erasmus (The Erasmus House)
Rotterdam: Gemeentebibliotheek Rotterdam
    (Rotterdam City Library; the Erasmus Collection
    can be consulted by appointment)

Websites

www.britannica.com/EBchecked/topic/191015/
    Desiderius-Erasmus
www.britannica.com/EBchecked/topic/275932/
    humanism
www.erasmus.org
www.erasmushouse.museum
www.quotes-of-wisdom.eu/en/home

Captions

[page 26] *Portrait of Erasmus*, Quinten Metsijs,
    The Royal Collection of H.M. The Queen,
    Buckingham Palace, London
[left] Illustration in the margin of *Praise of Folly*,
    Holbein the Younger, Kupferstichkabinett,
    Öffentliche Kunstsammlung, Basel
[right] Page from *Praise of Folly*, Library Collection,
    Rotterdam

1500 - 1558

Charles V

The Low Countries as an administrative unity

In the first half of the sixteenth century, the Low Countries consisted of different areas with their own laws and regulations. However, they had one thing in common: the Habsburg ruler Charles V. Charles's father, Duke Philip the Handsome, was a descendant of the Burgundians who had acquired a large number of dukedoms and counts' domains in the Low Countries in the late fourteenth century. His mother was heiress to the Spanish kingdoms of Aragon and Castile. Philip died when Charles was still young, so Charles had to ascend the throne early on in his life. In 1515 – at age fifteen – he became the ruler of the Low Countries; a year later he was also King of Spain and ruler of Spain's dominions in the New World; and in 1519 he was elected Emperor of the German empire.

This was the first time since Charlemagne that anyone had ruled over such a huge empire. Being emperor of an empire on which the sun never set created problems of its own. Confronted by hostile German princes, advancing Turks and a French king who mistrusted the expansion of the emperor's power, Charles moved from one war to the next. This cost a great deal of money that had to be supplied in part by the prosperous Low Countries. At the same time, Charles tried to make the Low Countries into an administrative unity and he conquered the last remaining independent provinces in the region: Frisland and Guelders.

This centralisation of politics was not welcomed by everyone. The towns resisted the high taxes and cherished their privileges, while the nobility defended their administrative functions against Charles's new civil servants. The presence of many supporters of the Reformation increased the tensions. Charles clung to the unity of the Church and took severe measures against dissidents: people who criticised the Roman Catholic Church created divisions. Charles had strict anti-heresy edicts proclaimed to the dismay of an ever-increasing group of town administrators and nobles who preached religious tolerance.

On 25 October 1555, in the golden hall of his Brussels palace, Charles abdicated his various positions. He was only fifty-five years old but he was burnt out from his administrative duties and gout.

Supported by the young prince William of Orange, he told those present of his love for the Low Countries, about the many efforts he had undertaken during his reign and of the mistakes he had made. He asked for forgiveness and begged those present to be as loyal to his successor, his son Philip II, as they had always been to him. Charles spent the last years of his life in a Spanish monastery where he died in 1558.

References

Places to Go
Brussels (Belgium): BELvue museum (a guided tour underneath the museum will let you discover the remains of Charles' palace)
Ghent (Belgium): The birthplace of Charles V

Websites
www.minbuza.nl/history/en/ontstaan,1515-1555.html
www.britannica.com/EBchecked/topic/107009/Charles-V
www.heksenwaag.nl
www.musbellevue.be/home.php

Captions
[page 28] *Charles V,* Titian, Alte Pinakothek, Munich/ The Bridgeman Art Library/XIR158620
[above] *Charles V on horseback,* Titian, Museo del Prado, Madrid

Nach wenigſh Predication   Das bildenſ ſtormen fiengen an   Kap Monſtrantz, kilch, auch die altar   Zerbrochen all in kurtzer ſtundt
Die Caluiniſche Religion   Das nicht ein bilde dauon bleib ſſan   Vnd weſſ ſonſt dort vor handen war,   Gleich gar vil leuten das iſt kunde .
                            Anno Diſ. M. D. LXVI̅J̅,J̅   XX   Auguſti

Li Borghesi d'Anversa avendo sentita la Predica del Calvinista cominciarono ad abbruggiare, e rompere, e saccheggiare le Chiese in Anversa.

1566

The *Beeldenstorm* (iconoclastic outbreak)
Religious conflict

Contemporary accounts refer to 1566 as the year of wonders. And indeed, the dramatic events that took place in quick succession made it a "wonderful" year. On 5 April, two hundred noble landowners presented a petition to Margaret, Duchess of Parma. The nobles wanted religious persecution to cease and a meeting of the States General to be held to discuss the country's problems. The Duchess was shocked by the numbers of the nobles but a councillor whispered in her ear: 'They are just "gueux" (beggars)'. Several days later, when the same nobles entered into an alliance with one another, they decided to call themselves "Beggars". In recognition of this name, from that time on they carried begging bowls attached to their belts and wore a special medal around their neck. Profiting from the indecision that was rampant in the administration of the country after the submission of their petition, the dissatisfied nobles offered increasingly open resistance in subsequent months, while supporters of the "new faith" gathered in public to listen to the sermons of travelling Calvinist preachers. On 10 August, one of these open-air sermons resulted in the plundering of a nearby monastery. This happened near Steenvoorde, in the Flemish Westhoek, the highly industrialised textile centre of the Low Countries. In the weeks and months that followed, other churches and monasteries were stormed and plundered, first in the rest of the Westhoek and then in other parts of Flanders and Brabant, and from the end of August, in the north of the Low Countries as well. With hindsight, there had been lots of omens. As a result of the severe persecution of heretics with the victims including ordinary, perfectly innocent men and women, unemployment and successive poor harvests, the situation had been inflammable for some time already. In the summer itself, the mood was predominantly one of surprise and astonishment and the wildest of rumours were rife.

The iconoclasts came from every layer of society. The high and low, rich and poor, male and female and young and old all stormed churches, destroyed images of saints and other works of art and plundered monasteries' stores. Their motives were as different as their backgrounds. Some hated the clergy with all their privileges, others were unhappy about their own meagre existence, while still others were simply curious, and the Calvinists believed the Church had to be purified of "papist superstitions". By drinking the communion wine, trampling consecrated wafers underfoot or feeding them to birds and smashing images of saints, they aimed to rid these Catholic symbols of their mystical value and make clear that Catholicism had been twisted into a sacrilegious puppet show of the

true faith. By purifying the churches of their images of saints, altars, works of art and other unnecessary luxuries, the Calvinists believed they were restoring ties with the earlier, in their eyes more pure, Christians and washing away centuries of corruption and the worship of false saints. The purified churches would be suitable from now on for reformed services in which the Word of God was the focal point: Bible reading and explanations of the Bible by a preacher.

References

Places to Go
Locally: Catholic and Protestant churches
Amsterdam: Oude Kerk (Old Church)
Utrecht: Museum Catharijneconvent

Websites
www.britannica.com/EBchecked/topic/232247/Geuzen
www.catharijneconvent.nl
dutchrevolt.leidenuniv.nl/English
www.minbuza.nl/history/en/ontstaan,1566.html
www.oudekerk.nl

Captions
[page 30] *Coloured engraving of the iconoclastic outbreak,* Hoogenbergh, Atlas Van Stolk, Rotterdam/AVS 50439(3)
[above] *De Beeldenstorm,* Dirk van Delen, Collection of the Rijksmuseum Amsterdam/ M-NG-2006-61-0

1533 - 1584

William of Orange

From rebel nobleman to "father of the country"

William of Orange was an ambitious nobleman who grew into a rebel leader and was later honoured as the "father of the country", as the founder of a new Dutch state. He himself had never envisaged the emergence of an independent state.

William was born in 1533 at Dillenburg Castle (in Germany). His parents were Lutheran, but when he inherited the principality of Orange (in France) in 1544 and could call himself "Prince", emperor Charles V insisted that the young prince be raised a Catholic. For this reason, from age twelve, William grew up at the royal court in Brussels. He was raised in the French language in his new surroundings in a manner that befitted his new standing.

From 1555 onwards, William of Orange acquired high positions. As a military commander, member of the Council of State, Knight of the Order of the Golden Fleece and Stadholder (governor) of Holland, Zeeland and Utrecht he was one of the most powerful noblemen in the Low Countries. However, his relationship with Philip II, Charles V's successor, quickly deteriorated. William became the major spokesman of the noble opposition party. They were arguing for the persecution of heretics to be scaled down and they resisted the rise of professional civil servants in the administration of the country. The rise of the new civil servants meant that the nobility were losing their traditional positions.

After the debacle of the iconoclastic outbreak, William fled to Dillenburg. From here, from 1568 onwards, he undertook several military assaults on the Low Countries to bring to an end the rule of Duke of Alva. He also used propaganda (pamphlets, battle songs and cartoons) in this battle. One of the products of this period is the Dutch national anthem, the Wilhelmus. William had little initial success. Only when the Sea Beggars took Den Briel by accident on 1 April 1572 did the Rebellion begin to receive widespread support.

Against all expectations, the rebels in Holland and Zeeland continued to hold fast, due in part to the perseverance of William of Orange. With the Pacification of Ghent in 1576 the rebels even managed to make peace with the various provinces. The ideals of William of Orange seemed within reach: the restoration of the seventeen Burgundian Low Countries under the administration of the nobles, and the resolution of the prevailing religious differences, based on tolerance. However, the new unity did not last.

In 1580, Philip II placed a bounty on the head of William of Orange. William's response was to write an *Apologie* (defence) and the States General of the rebelling provinces responded with a *Plakkaat van verlatinghe* (Oath of Abjuration). Both these documents had the same message: resistance was justified because the king was acting like a tyrant. On 10 July 1584 a Catholic, Balthasar Gerards, shot William of Orange and brought an end to his life. William appeared to have achieved nothing, but less than twenty-five years later the rebellious provinces had developed into a self-confident Republic and William of Orange was regarded as the founding father of the new state.

33

References

Places to Go

Alkmaar: Stedelijk Museum
   (Alkmaar City Museum; Siege of Alkmaar)
Breda: Kasteel van Breda
   (castle; court of the Nassau family in Breda)
Brielle: Historisch Museum 'Den Briel'
   (Historical Museum) and city walk (1572)
Buren: Museum Buren & Oranje
Delft: Stedelijk Museum Het Prinsenhof
Delft: the tomb of William of Orange in
   the Nieuwe Kerk (New Church)
Leiden: Stedelijk Museum 'De Lakenhal'
   (Leiden City Museum; Siege of Leiden)
Dillenburg (Germany): 'Wilhelmsturm'
   and Orange Museum

Websites

www.britannica.com/EBchecked/topic/644041/William-I
http://dutchrevolt.leidenuniv.nl
www.historischmuseumdenbriel.nl
www.inghist.nl/Onderzoek/Projecten/WVO/
   en/index_html
www.koninklijkhuis.nl/english
www.lakenhal.nl/en
www.minbuza.nl/history/en/ontstaan,1568.html
www.nieuwekerk-delft.nl
www.zuid-hollandse-eilanden.nl

Captions

[page 32] *Portrait of William of Orange,*
   Adriaen Thomasz. Key, Collection of the
   Rijksmuseum Amsterdam/SK-A-3148
[above] *The murder of William of Orange,* Hoogenbergh,
   Atlas van Stolk, Rotterdam/AVS 806

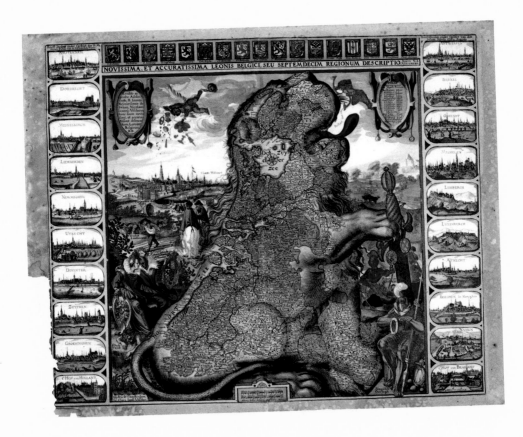

1588 - 1795

The Republic

A unique political phenomenon

In 1609, the Twelve-Year Truce resulted in a temporary cessation of the war with Spain that had begun in 1568 with the military attacks of William of Orange. To commemorate the occasion, Claes Janszoon Visscher produced a map of the Low Countries in the shape of a lion, the *Leo Belgicus*. The map depicts the seventeen low countries as a unity, existing peacefully side by side thanks to the silencing of the guns, symbolised by the sleeping figure of Mars at the bottom right. In truth, however, the Low Countries had been split into two states by the Rebellion and the subsequent war: the southern, Spanish Low Countries and the northern Republic of the Seven United Low Countries. The latter had recorded a diplomatic success with the Truce even though international recognition as a sovereign state would only come in 1648 with the signing of the Treaty of Westphalia in Munster.

Republics were the exception to the rule in early-modern Europe where princes set the tone. Therefore, none of the rebels had actually been aiming to establish a republic: they had simply wanted to bring back "the good old days" when princes had guaranteed the freedoms and privileges of towns, provinces and subjects. Such a prince had been sought after the renunciation of Philip II, but had not been found. For this reason, in 1588 the seven remaining rebellious provinces took the form of a republic.

This resulted in a remarkable system of government in which, in theory, each province had an equal voice in the general meetings of the States General. Members had the right of consultation. This meant that delegates had to return to their provinces for consultation. Consequently, it could take a long time for decisions to be made. In practice the system was not too bad. Given that the wealthy province of Holland provided the most revenue, it also had the greatest say. The highest official of Holland, the Grand Pensionary, had duties similar to President of the Republic, Minister of Finance and Minister of Foreign Affairs all rolled into one. In addition, a member of the House of Orange usually held the office of *Stadholder* (governor). The Dutch term literally means "deputy" or "replacement", but this was

now simply a reference to early times: after all, there was now no liege lord who had to be replaced. As a high nobleman from the House of Oranje-Nassau (and therefore a descendant of William of Orange) and commander of the armed forces, the *Stadholder* was positioned well above all other administrators and officials. Whereas such civil servants spent their time largely in meetings, *Stadholders* like Maurice and Frederik Hendrik recorded military successes against the Spanish. They had something of the air of a prince about them, even though they were officially simply servants of the County Council.

The *Stadholder* and *Grand Pensionary* could easily come into conflict with one another. During the Twelve Year Truce, this happened for the first time, with a dramatic outcome. After a heated political and religious conflict, *Stadholder* Maurice had Johan van Oldenbarneveldt arrested on the charge of high treason. Oldenbarneveldt was sent to the block on 13 May 1619.

References

Places to Go

Amsterdam: Koninklijk Paleis op de Dam
 (City Hall/ Royal Palace Amsterdam)
Gouda: Grote of Sint-Janskerk, 'Goudse Glazen'
 (church with stained-glass windows,
 partly dating from the sixteenth century)
The Hague: Binnenhof and surroundings

Websites

www.binnenhofbezoek.nl
www.britannica.com/EBchecked/topic/620843/
 Union-of-Utrecht
www.britannica.com/EBchecked/topic/174609/
 Dutch-Republic
http://dutchrevolt.leidenuniv.nl
www.koninklijkhuis.nl/english
www.minbuza.nl/history/en/ontstaan,1579.html
www.sintjan.com

Captions

[page 34] *Leo Belgica,* Atlas Van Stolk, Rotterdam/
 AVS 1248

1602 - 1799

The Dutch East India Company (VOC)
Overseas expansion

Mauritius, Hollandia and Amsterdam, these were the names of the three merchant ships that set sail from Texel for "the East", together with the small ship the Duyfken, on 2 April 1595. It proved to be an exciting adventure. Only three of the four vessels returned in August 1597 and only 87 of the 249-man crew. The revenues were modest. But still, this first Dutch sailing expedition to Asia was a success because it opened a trade route to the East.

Other expeditions followed. With their strong and heavily armed trading vessels the merchant traders from Zeeland and Holland out-performed the Portuguese who had used the route for some time, and the English became jealous. The ships returned heavily laden with colonial goods like pepper and nutmeg. To limit internal competition, Johan van Oldenbarneveldt took the initiative of setting up the Dutch East India Company (VOC). On 20 March 1602, the company acquired the Dutch monopoly on all trade in Asian waters from the Cape of Good Hope onwards. The company was empowered to sign treaties in the name of the Republic, to wage war and administer conquered territories.

The VOC developed into a power to be feared. 'This can lead to something big,' wrote Jan Pieterszoon Coen to the Heren

XVII, the board of the VOC in the distant fatherland. In 1619, he conquered the town of Jayakarta and founded Batavia there. Coen wrote that '*Jacatra*' would become 'the most important place in all the Indies' and that the reputation of the Dutch had increased through their conquests. 'Everyone will now seek to become our friend'. Parts of Java were occupied, Ambon and Ternate in the Mulluccas were subjugated and the population was forced to cultivate spices. Elsewhere in Asia too the VOC gained ground with either persuasion or violence. Forts were built in South Africa, India, Ceylon (Sri Lanka) and Makassar in Indonesia. China was visited and when in 1641 the Shogun of Japan closed his country's borders to foreigners, the VOC alone received his permission to continue to trade from the island of Decima near Nagasaki.

In this way, the VOC not only stocked Dutch warehouses with colonial goods and filled the houses of the bourgeois with curiosa from foreign lands, but they also played an important trading role within Asia. Textiles, spices, coffee, tea, tobacco, opium, tropical wood, iron, copper, silver, gold, porcelain, dyes, shells – an endless array of goods was transported by the Dutch East India fleet.

In 1799, in the time of the French, the VOC was dissolved. Today, the archives of the VOC are regarded as world heritage, a *memory of the world*. The daily reports of the merchants who organised trade from the forts, the reports of the travels of VOC officials to royal courts of rulers with whom they traded, ships' bills of lading... together the documents are an important source of information about two centuries of Asian-European history.

References

Places to Go
Amsterdam, Delft and Middelburg:
  city walks on the subject of the VOC
Amsterdam: Amsterdams Historisch Museum
  (Amsterdam Historical Museum)
Amsterdam: Nederlands Scheepvaartmuseum Amsterdam
  (National Maritime Museum Amsterdam;
  replica VOC ship)
Amsterdam: Tropenmuseum
Delft: Nusantara Museum (museum about
  the history and cultures of Indonesia)
Leiden: Museum Volkenkunde
  (National Museum of Ethnology)
Lelystad: Bataviawerf
Utrecht: Museum Maluku ((history of) Moluccan
  community in the Netherlands)
Rotterdam: Maritiem Museum Rotterdam
  (Maritime Museum Rotterdam)
Rotterdam: Scheepswerf 'De Delft'
  (shipyard; the building of a reconstruction
  of an eighteenth-century Dutch ship)
Vlissingen: Maritiem MuZEEum Vlissingen (Maritime
  MuZEEum Vlissingen; large collection of objects from
  the VOC ship 't Vliegent Hart, which sunk in 1735)

Websites
www.bataviawerf.nl
www.britannica.com/EBchecked/topic/174553/
  Dutch-East-Indies
www.britannica.com/EBchecked/topic/174523/
  Dutch-East-India-Company
www.koninklijkhuis.nl/english
www.maritiemmuseum.nl
www.minbuza.nl/history/en/oorlog,1602.html
www.museum-maluku.nl
www.rmv.nl
www.scheepvaartmuseum.nl
www.tropenmuseum.nl

Captions
[page 36] *Replica of the Batavia*, Batavia shipyard –
  Nationaal Scheepshistorisch Centrum/Jaap Roskam

1612

The Beemster Polder

The Netherlands and water

There is a good reason for the fact that the Beemster Polder is listed on the Unesco World Heritage Register. The draining of this lake in 1612 is a shining example of how the Dutch "created" large areas of their country in the north, west and south-west of the Netherlands. The Netherlands took shape by man battling the elements. It started with small-scale land reclamation and the building of dykes in the Middle Ages. The scale became increasing larger from the sixteenth century onwards with the draining of lakes and peat bogs, and, for the time being, work was wound up in the twentieth century with the laying down of the Flevo polders and the Maasvlakte.

In 1607, a group of Amsterdam merchants and town administrators decided to drain the Beemster which at the time was a large lake. It promised to be a finan-cially lucrative project that moreover would contribute to providing food for the fast-growing town of Amsterdam. A high, strong dyke with a length of 38 kilometres was built around the lake; around that dyke, the ring canal was dug. After this, work began on pumping the lake dry, using no fewer than 43 windmills. An engineer, Jan Adriaenszoon Leeghwater, was responsible for the building and placement of the windmills. A series of mills had to be built, each slightly higher than the last, so that the water was gradually pumped into the ring canal.

In 1612, the lake was dry and the polder could be laid out. Roads were laid, channels and ditches were dug and farms were built. The design was well-ordered in a tight geometric pattern. The Beemster Polder's fame is due to this parcellation and design.

Over the centuries, a great deal of tinkering was done to the system of water management in the Beemster. For a long time it was the windmills that had to ensure that the residents kept their feet dry and that the water levels were suitable for land cultivation. In the late nineteenth century, the windmills were replaced by steam-driven pumping stations, and later still by diesel and electric-driven pumps. Today, the Beemster is divided into over fifty sections, each with its own water level. Farmers need a low water level under their land, while village residents want a high level to prevent the posts under their houses from rotting on contact with air. The ideal water level for cattle farmers is somewhere in between, while nature conservationists have their own requirements.

In the past, water was only pumped away to prevent flooding but today, in dry periods, water is also pumped into the Beemster. This is possible because the IJsselmeer, the former Zuiderzee, now contains fresh water of a quality suitable for agriculture.

The power of the wind and windmills once allowed the Beemster waters to be drained and land to be reclaimed. Today electricity and computers are used to manage the water levels.

References

Places to Go

Beemster: a walk along the ring dike gives the visitor a good view of the straight, strict lines of the exceptional land divisionand the typical shapes of the "stolp" farms

Cruquius: Museum De Cruquius (former steam pumping station)

Middenbeemster: Infocentrum Beemster (information centre about the Beemster)

Middenbeemster: Museum Betje Wolff

Websites

www.beemsterinfo.nl/index_04.htm
www.beemsterswelvaart.nl/vogelvlucht/engels.htm
www.museumdecruquius.nl/en/index.html
www.watermuseum.nl
http://whc.unesco.org/en/list/899

Captions

[page 38] *Windmill,* Frans Heijn

[left] *Aerial photograph of the Beemster,* Pandion/ Peter Bolhuis

[right] *Working drawing of a typical Beemster mill, from "Groot volkomen Moolenboek",* unknown

1613 - 1662

The canal ring

Urban development in the seventeenth century

On aerial photographs and maps, the Amsterdam canal ring is immediately recognisable due to its characteristic semi-circular form made up of the Herengracht, Keizersgracht and Prinsengracht canals in the centre of the city. The canal ring is a fine example of Dutch urban development in the seventeenth century. With the massive inflow of new arrivals in the prosperous western Republic from the end of the sixteenth century onwards, town administrators and town-dwellers were confronted with overcrowded towns, housing shortages and a lack of space. Urban development was unavoidable. But how could this be realised and what should the priorities be? Should the starting point be sensible considerations or aesthetic principles as set out in the popular tracts on the ideal city?

At the end of the sixteenth century, the city of Amsterdam made a cautious start at increasing urban space.

Large-scale development, however, only took place from 1613 onwards when the three canals mentioned above were dug up to the current Leidsegracht. A new western port area was realised by the creation of three rectangular islands and a new neighbourhood was developed to the west of the canals: the Jordaan. This was all done in accordance with a master plan involving various parties: the town administration, the Stadholder (governor), the Council of Holland and the town carpenter, Hendrick Jacobszoon Staets. It was a large project. Land had to be repossessed, new defences had to be built and funds had to be made available to finance the undertaking.

The elements of functionality and beauty were combined in the plan. Wherever possible, use was made of tight geometric shapes, which means the urban development features the consistent use of straight lines. In addition, the aim was to create a geographic division between the various urban functions. The new western islands mainly accommodated wharves and shipping companies, whereas the Jordaan district provided room for housing and small businesses. The canals had an exclusively residential function. Numerous "urban palaces" arose, built by wealthy merchants, bankers, town administrators and other men of means.

In the period from 1656 to 1662, the canals were extended to across the river Amstel, which gave the centre of Amsterdam its current shape. The design continued along the lines of the first phase: new, even more lovely and bigger canal houses decorated this new section. Today, the Golden Bend of the Herengracht can still be regarded as a symbol of the wealth of the Golden Age.

At the time of this last development the Golden Age was drawing to a close. The development of 1662 had been too optimistic. The newly-won urban area to the east of the Amstel remained noticeably empty until far into the nineteenth century.

Today, the canal ring serves as a familiar example of typically Dutch urbanisation. The urban waterways, the small scale, the innumerable bicycles, the bustling city centre, these are the hallmarks of a true Dutch city.

References

Places to Go
Amsterdam: a walk along the Canals
Amsterdam: Amsterdams Historisch Museum (Amsterdam Historical Museum, which offers a combination in guided tours through the city and in the museum every last Saturday of the month)
Amsterdam: Woonbootmuseum (Houseboat Museum)

Websites
www.amsterdamtourist.nl/en
www.houseboatmuseum.nl
www.vvvamsterdam.nl

Captions
[page 40] *Herengracht*, Frans Heijn
[above] *Amsterdam canal*, Andrew Ward/Life File, Getty Images

1583 - 1645

Hugo Grotius

Pioneer of modern international law

Hugo Grotius was well known to the public at large mainly because of the book chest which he used to escape from Loevestein Castle on 22 March 1621. He had been imprisoned in the castle in 1619 for treason. As Pensionary of Rotterdam and political and legal advisor to government prosecutor Oldenbarneveldt, Grotius was one of the leading players in the Truce Negotiations. After the fall of Oldenbarneveldt, Grotius's days were numbered. Although (unlike his protector) he was not executed, he was sentenced to a life in prison. Thanks to the ruse with the book chest he did not serve his full term. He did, however, have to spend the rest of his life in exile abroad. Grotius died in 1645 in Rostock.

In 1621, Hugo Grotius's time in Holland came to an end but his intellectual activities and academic reputation continued to grow. He had earned his reputation early

in life. A child prodigy, Grotius was born in 1583 in Delft and at age eleven he was admitted to the newly established University of Leiden. Here, he was hailed as the successor of Erasmus. The young Grotius had an unparalleled intellect. He could write Latin verses as easily as he could write annotations to ancient Greek and Roman texts. In 1598 the French king referred to him as "the Dutch miracle".

Hugo Grotius remained a man of many talents for the rest of his life. He wrote discourses on theological, historical, and, in particular, legal topics. Initially, his Dutch roots could be clearly seen in his writing. For example, using a flood of historical and legal examples he tried to prove that Holland had had the ideal form of government since the time of the Batavians, or that the Dutch were free to use the seas as these were international waters (*Mare Liberum*). The way in which he reached these conclusions was typical for humanist scholars like Grotius. Using his astonishing scholarship, his primary aim was to bring order and structure to existing knowledge as could be found in the works of classical writers. This approach delivered important new insights, particularly in his legal writings like *De iure belli ac pacis* ("On the law of war and peace"). Written in 1625, this work sets out the fundamental principles of international law.

In the Netherlands, Grotius is known as Hugo de Groot, and is still largely remembered for the tale of the book chest. Abroad, the name Grotius is associated with a man with a brilliant legal mind. Together with his fellow victims of the Stadholder (the De Witt brothers and Oldenbarneveldt), Hugo Grotius served as a symbol of resistance for the opponents of the Orangists. During the 1780s, the Patriot period, several relics of Grotius came to light, including two book chests.

References

Places to Go
Delft: Nieuwe Kerk (New Church: Grotius is buried here and a memorial is erected to him; outside the church there is a statue of Grotius)
Poederoijen: Slot Loevestein (Loevestein Castle)
The Hague: Vredespaleis (Peace Palace: its Library has the most extensive collection of works by Grotius in the world)

Websites
www.britannica.com/EBchecked/topic/246809/ Hugo-Grotius
www.nieuwekerk-delft.nl
www.vredespaleis.nl

Captions
[page 42] *The book chest of Hugo Grotius,* Collection of the Rijksmuseum Amsterdam/NG-KOG-1208
[left] *Portrait of Hugo Grotius,* Michiel Jansz. van Miereveld, Collection of the Rijksmuseum Amsterdam
[right] *Aerial photograph of Loevestein Castle,* Loevestein Castle

1637
The *Statenbijbel*
(authorised version of the Bible)
The Book of Books

For Christians, the Bible is the most important book in existence because it contains the truth revealed by God, "the word of God". One of the points of conflict during the Reformation had been the question of for whom the Bible was meant. The Catholic Church believed that the Bible should preferably not be read by ordinary people. Rather, they could listen to the explanations of the clergy in church, where the priests read from the Bible in Latin. The priests acted as inter-mediaries between God and the faithful.

The protestants, on the other hand, believed that the faithful themselves should be able to read the Bible and that the preacher in the first place was a servant of the word of God. It was the task of preachers to let God's word speak to the congregation, through Bible readings and exegis of the Scriptures. This meant,

therefore, that the Bible should be available in the language of the faithful, preferably in as reliable a translation as possible. Consequently, the reformer Luther translated the Bible from the original texts into German in around 1535. In the sixteenth century, a number of Dutch translations were made of Luther's German work.

Over the course of time, the call from the Dutch Reformed Church became ever stronger for a new translation based on the original manuscripts of the Bible in Hebrew and Greek. In 1618, the synod of the Dutch Reformed Church, during its main assembly in the city of Dordrecht, commissioned such a translation based on the example of the English Authorised Version (the King James Bible of 1611). The States General was asked to finance the translation.

The States General only agreed to this in 1626 and the translators were then able to start work. Nine years later the translation was completed, and in 1637 the Dutch authorised version, the *Statenvertaling* or *Statenbijbel*, was printed for the first time. Over 500,000 copies were printed between 1637 and 1657. The *Statenbijbel* remained the most important Bible in the Dutch Reformed Church for over three hundred years. Even today it is still used in some church communities. Currently, work is being done on a revised version of the *Statenvertaling*.

Over the course of time, through sermons and Bible readings, large groups of people became familiar with the language of the *Statenbijbel*, that also had an enormous impact on Dutch culture. The *Statenvertaling* was the source for expressions like "in the sweat of thy face" and "a feast for the eye", that have now become embedded in the Dutch language.

45

References

Places to Go

Amsterdam: Bijbels museum (Biblical Museum)
Amsterdam: Joods Historisch Museum
    (Jewish Historical Museum)
Heilig Landstichting (near Nijmegen):
    Museumpark Orientalis
Leerdam: Statenbijbelmuseum (States Bible Museum;
    collection of restored Dutch (States) Bibles dating
    from the sixteenth to the twentieth century)
Uden: Museum voor Religieuze Kunst
    (Museum for Religious Art)
Utrecht: Museum Catharijneconvent

Websites

www.bijbelsmuseum.nl
www.britannica.com/EBchecked/topic/564027/
    States-Bible
www.catharijneconvent.nl
www.jhm.nl
www.museumparkorientalis.nl
www.statenvertaling.net/english.html
www.catharijneconvent.nl

Captions

[page 44] *Statenbijbel*, Platvorm BV
[left] *Title page of the Statenbijbel*, Collection of the
    Catherijneconvent, Utrecht
[right] *Old woman reading from a lectionarium*, Gerard Dou,
    Collection of the Rijksmuseum Amsterdam/SK-A-2627

1606? - 1669

Rembrandt

The great painters

Rembrandt van Rijn's painting "The Night Watch" is world famous. The painting dates from 1642 and since that time it has been commented on, praised and discussed on innumerable occasions. It is indeed an intriguing painting: it depicts something – but what? On the other hand, it is an ordinary painting: a group of Amsterdam residents depicted as members of the civic guard around their Captain Frans Banning Cocq. The painting was intended to be hung in the new great hall of the renovated Kloveniersdoelen (the headquarters of the civic guardsmen). Such group portraits belonged to a tradition that dated back to the first half of the sixteenth century. Banning Cocq's

colleagues did themselves equal justice: they too commissioned group portraits by well-known artists. Rembrandt's painting therefore originally hung in the company of a number of other recent group portraits in the new Doelenzaal of the Kloveniersdoelen where the guardsmen regularly met to eat, drink and smoke together.

At the time that Banning Cocq commissioned Rembrandt, the latter was already much in demand as a portrait painter. He was also ambitious and had left his birthplace (Leiden) at an early age in the hope of making a better career for himself in the richer, larger town of Amsterdam. He was successful. With his expensive portraits and paintings of biblical and mythological figures and stories, Rembrandt served the elite among the wealthy bourgeoisie and art lovers.

The Amsterdam art market was, however, much wider in scope. Around the year 1650, the city had some 175 artists. The majority of them produced cheap paintings for an anonymous market, mainly small landscapes and so-called genre pieces depicting everyday scenes. These painters did not achieve eternal fame, but their work is a mark of the wealth and scope of seventeenth-century Dutch painting. Spurred on by the great demand from ordinary citizens for paintings to decorate their homes, all over the Republic artists tried to create their own niche in the market. It has been calculated that in the seventeenth century over five million paintings must have been produced. This figure clearly illustrates that Dutch painting was not dominated by a few great masters working in important artistic centres such as Amsterdam, Haarlem and Utrecht. It is therefore not Rembrandt alone who symbolises the remarkable cultural boom of the seventeenth century, but also the hundreds of second and third-rate local painters who tried to make a living in the shadows of famous masters or working in smaller artistic centres like Enkhuizen and Zwolle.

47

References

Places to Go
Alkmaar: Stedelijk Museum Alkmaar
 (Alkmaar City Museum)
Amsterdam: Amsterdams Historisch Museum
 (Amsterdam Historical Museum; paintings of
 guildmembers of 'schutterijen')
Amsterdam: Museum het Rembrandthuis
 (Rembrandt House Museum)
Amsterdam: Rijksmuseum
Delft: Vermeer Centrum Delft (Vermeer Centre Delft)
Haarlem: Frans Hals Museum
Leiden: Stedelijk Museum De Lakenhal
 (Leiden City Museum)
The Hague: Mauritshuis

Websites
www.britannica.com/EBchecked/topic/497584/
 Rembrandt
www.mauritshuis.nl
www.minbuza.nl/history/en/1600tot1700,1600---1700.html
www.rembrandthuis.com
www.rijksmuseum.nl/meesterwerken

Captions
[page 46] *Het korporaalschap van kapitein Frans
 Banninck Cocq en luitenant Willem van Ruytenburch/
 The Night Watch,* Rembrandt Harmensz. van Rijn,
 Collection of the Rijksmuseum Amsterdam/SK-C-5
[right] *Self Portrait as the Apostle St. Paul,* Rembrandt
 Harmensz. van Rijn, Collection of the Rijksmuseum
 Amsterdam/SK-A-4050

1662
Blaeu's *Atlas Major*
Mapping the world

In the seventeenth century, the Blaeu family was world famous for the atlases and maps printed by their family business in Amsterdam. The Republic was enjoying its Golden Age and Amsterdam was steadily growing as a centre of international trade, overseas expansion and wealth. Such a town provided the international contacts, the financial resources and the market for starting a thriving printing business in maps and atlases. Not only were there sufficient mariners and merchants who needed reliable navigation tools, also many wealthy members of the bourgeoisie appeared to be curious about the world beyond the horizon. They were prepared to pay for luxury editions of atlases or beautiful globes of the earth and the heavens.

This was not a completely new market. In the last decades of the sixteenth century, based on examples from abroad, cartographers in Enkhuizen and Edam had searched for suitable maps for mariners and other interested citizens. Willem Janszoon Blaeu responded to this demand, making good use of his knowledge of the subject and sound business instincts. After an apprenticeship with the famous Danish astronomer Tycho Brahe, Blaeu set up a printer's and publishing house in Amsterdam. His first printed maps date from 1605 and he distinguished himself from the outset by the quality and innovations in his work. Blaeu did not go out to take measurements himself. He designed his maps based on existing cartographic material, supplemented by the knowledge he drew from ships' logs, travel journals and talks with mariners. His maps and atlases gained Blaeu an international reputation.

After his death in 1638, his son Joan took over the business. Joan expanded the family business still further and published numerous new maps and atlases, including the renowned *Atlas Major*, that was brought onto the market from 1662 onwards in various editions and languages. This multi-volume atlas maps the known world of the time in six hundred maps and several thousand pages of descriptions. The atlas illustrated how knowledge of the world had been increased by voyages of discovery and trade contacts. At the same time, the atlas was a desirable status symbol, print-ed in folio format and bound in expensive leather if so desired. The maps themselves were beautifully printed but seldom original. Often, they had been published previously, sometimes they were outdated and they were largely inaccurate. However, all this had hardly any effect on the esteem in which the atlas was held. With his *Atlas Major* Blaeu had brought the known world within hands' reach in the loveliest way possible.

49

References

Places to Go

Amsterdam: Amsterdams Historisch Museum
   (Amsterdam Historical Museum)
Amsterdam: Nationaal Scheepvaartmuseum Amsterdam
   (National Maritime Museum Amsterdam)
Leeuwarden: TRESOAR (Friesland Historical and
   Literary Centre)
Rotterdam: Maritiem Museum Rotterdam
   (Maritime Museum Rotterdam)

Websites

www.kb.nl/galerie/100hoogtepunten
www.leidenarchief.nl/component/option,com_album
   (digitally available version of *Toonneel des Aerdriicx,
   ofte Nieuwe Atlas* by Joan Blaeu, web page in Dutch)
www.scheepvaartmuseum.nl/english

Captions

[page 48] *Theatre of the World, or a New Atlas of
   Maps and Representations of All Regions,*
   Willem and Joan Blaeu, Universiteitsbibliotheek UvA,
   Bijzondere Collecties
[left] *Hollandia 1604,* Blaeu, Universiteitsbibliotheek UvA,
   Bijzondere Collecties
[right] *Frontispiece from Blaeu's Theatrum,*
   Blaeu Sr. and Jr., 1648, unknown

1607 - 1676
Michiel de Ruyter
Heroes of the sea and the wide reach of the Republic

The Republic was at war for a large part of the seventeenth century. In 1648, the Eighty Years' War with the Spanish came to an end with the signing of the Treaty of Westphalia in Munster. However, the Republic did not enjoy peace for long. Conflicting trade interests quickly led to two sea wars with England (from 1652-1654 and from 1665-1667). In 1672, the English and the French launched a combined attack on the Republic that brought it to the brink of destruction. It managed to survive, however, and in the decades that followed the Republic played an important role in the international coalition that resisted the territorial ambitions of the French king Louis XIV.

In the meantime, the administrators of the coastal provinces presented the image of the Republic as a peace-loving maritime and trade nation that only waged war with the greatest reluctance to protect its economic interests. The great heroes in this self-made image were the admirals of the fleet and their sailors. Songs were written about them, their lives and deeds were set down in popular history booklets and major sea battles were depicted in paintings and prints. Fleet admirals who died in battle were assured of a magnificent mausoleum.

Michiel Adriaenszoon de Ruyter is without doubt the most famous of all seventeenth-century heroes of the sea. He was born in Vlissingen in 1607, the son of a humble beer porter. From early on it was clear that his future lay on the seas. After working for some time as a rope-maker for the Lampsins, the wealthiest family of ship owners in Vlissingen, in 1618 he signed on as an orderly for the Chief Petty Officer on his first ship. It was the beginning of an adventurous life on the seas. As a privateer captain, rear admiral and merchantman he sailed the world's oceans and tried his luck.

In 1652, he believed he had acquired sufficient wealth to lead a tranquil life on shore. However, De Ruyter did not enjoy his rest for long. After the outbreak of the First Anglo-Dutch War, the Admiralty of Zeeland offered him a position. De Ruyter accepted, for one voyage. However, this soon appeared to be the start of a new career culminating in his appointment to the highest position in the navy, that of Lieutenant-Admiral.

De Ruyter's greatest moment came in 1667, at the height of the Second Anglo-Dutch War. On the urging of Grand Pensionary Johan de Witt, De Ruyter sailed his fleet up the Thames and into the Medway, inflicting an embarrassing defeat on the English on their own soil. A large part of the English fleet was destroyed on the Medway near Chatham. De Ruyter was hailed as the new Hannibal.

In 1676, De Ruyter died in a battle against the French near Syracuse. It was to have been his last expedition. He was buried in a marble mausoleum on the spot where the high altar had formerly stood in the Nieuwe Kerk in Amsterdam.

References

Places to Go

Amsterdam: Nationaal Scheepvaartmuseum Amsterdam
  (National Maritime Museum Amsterdam)
Amsterdam: Nieuwe Kerk
  (New Church: tomb of Michiel de Ruyter)
Amsterdam: Rijksmuseum
Rotterdam: Maritiem Museum Rotterdam
  (Maritime Museum Rotterdam)
Vlissingen: Maritiem MuZEEum Vlissingen
  (Maritime MuZEEum Vlissingen)
Vlissingen: De Ruyter-wandeling
  (walk on the subject of De Ruyter)

Websites

www.bataviawerf.nl
www.britannica.com/EBchecked/topic/514375/
  Michiel-Adriaanszoon-De-Ruyter
www.deruyter.org/ENGLISH_SECTION.html
www.maritiemmuseum.nl
www.muzeeum.nl
www.nieuwekerk.nl
www.rijksmuseum.nl
www.scheepvaartmuseum.nl/english

Captions

[page 50] *Portrait of Michiel Adriaenszoon de Ruyter,* Ferdinand Bol, Collection of the Rijksmuseum Amsterdam/SK-A-44
[above] *The court martial aboard the Seven Provinces,* Willem van de Velde Senior, Rijksmuseum, Amsterdam/SK-A-4289

1629-1695

Christiaan Huygens

Science in the Golden Age

Christiaan Huygens, born in 1629, was the second son of the poet Constantijn Huygens who was secretary to two Princes of Orange. Christiaan Huygens' father had envisaged diplomatic careers for his sons and he therefore sent them to study law, first in Leiden and later in Breda. However, Christiaan was more interested in maths, physics and astronomy. As a child he refused to write verses in Latin. He preferred to tinker with tiny windmills and other model machines and to observe the ripples created by throwing a stone into water.

At an early age, Christiaan was already corresponding about various issues with authoritative scholars abroad. In 1647, the French philosopher, physicist and mathematician Mersenne wrote to Christiaan's father: "If he continues in this way he will one day even surpass Archimedes." For the rest of his days

Constantijn Huygens referred to his son as "my Archimedes".

Huygens was a regular visitor to England and France too, where in 1655 he was awarded a doctorate and was appointed the first director of the Royal Academy of Science in 1666. This appointment illustrates the international attention Huygens' work attracted. From 1681 up until his death, Huygens lived either in Voorburg (in the Hofwijck summer residence designed by his father) or on the Plein (town square) in the centre of The Hague.

Christiaan was an admirer of Descartes, the "father of modern philosophy" who did not base his thinking on doctrines and theories that had been handed down across generations. He wanted to perform experiments himself, to observe and formulate laws. This new form of scientific practice became known as the Scientific

Revolution. And this was exactly what Huygens did: he constantly observed, experimented and monitored.

Christiaan's achievements lay in many fields: in mathematics, he wrote about squaring the circle, among other things. In physics, he studied free fall and pendulum motion and the pendulum clock – his best-known achievement – was a result of these studies (1656). Christiaan Huygens also worked at improving sea clocks so that they would keep as accurate time as possible on ships at sea and would not stop. Knowing the precise time was of great importance in determining the position of ships at sea.

Together with his brother Constantijn (his elder by thirteen months) with whom he corresponded frequently and to whom he was very close, Christiaan began to grind lenses for microscopes and astronomical telescopes. He discovered the ring of Saturn with such a telescope and just before that (in 1655) Titan, the first moon of a planet ever to be discovered. The peculiar phenomena around Saturn had been described by earlier scholars as some kind of "ears" of the heavenly body. Christiaan revealed the true situation and reported his findings to many authoritative astronomers in Europe. Regarding Saturn's ring and the moon Titan he wrote: "These remain signs of my ingenuity and the names I have written across the heavens will still echo my fame long after my death."

53

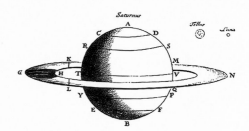

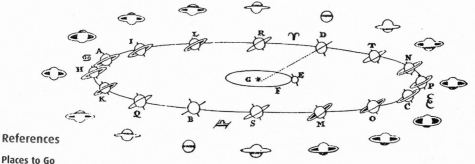

References

Places to Go
Amsterdam: NEMO
Leiden: Museum Boerhaave (Boerhaave Museum)
Voorburg: Huygensmuseum Hofwijck

Websites
www.britannica.com/EBchecked/topic/277775
www.e-nemo.nl
www.hofwijck.nl
www.museumboerhaave.nl

Captions
[page 52] *Constantijn Huygens and his five children (detail, Christiaan Huygens),* Adriaen Hanneman, Koninklijk Kabinet van Schilderijen Mauritshuis, Den Haag

[above] Drawings of Saturn by Christiaan Huygens (1659) and a photo of Saturn made by the NASA Cassini-Huygens mission in 2004

1632 - 1677

Spinoza

In search of truth

Spinoza is the most famous philosopher of the Netherlands: he belongs to a small group of philosophers who changed the course of western thinking.

Benedictus de Spinoza was born in Amsterdam in 1632 as Baruch d'Espinoza, the son of Jewish parents who had fled from Portugal. He died in The Hague in 1677 of a lung disease. Spinoza lived a quite frugal life and to earn his keep he ground lenses for glasses and microscopes. His illness was probably aggravated by the dust he inhaled in this work.

Spinoza's nickname was "Bento", which means the same in Portuguese as Baruch in Hebrew and Benedictus in Latin: "the blessed". Spinoza learned Dutch, Portuguese, Spanish and Hebrew and later wrote in Latin. After his religious training, in 1656 he came into conflict with the Amsterdam Jewish community. Probably not because he was critical of orthodox beliefs, but rather because he did not want to conform outwardly to the strict orthodox rules and requirements.

Although in comparison with surrounding countries the Republic was tolerant and dealt patiently with criticism, Spinoza still had to be careful. He published a lot of his works under a pseudonym – or not at all. His major work, the *Ethica*, was only published after his death.

In the "disaster year" of 1672, the atmosphere became increasingly turbulent and the De Witt brothers were lynched by an Orangist mob without any interference from the authorities. This shocked Spinoza so deeply that he wanted to take a placard to the spot bearing the text *ultimi barbarorum* ('you are the greatest of all barbarians'). His landlord and friend stopped him and in so doing probably saved his life.

In his book *Tractatus theologico-politicus* Spinoza gave the initial impetus to a free-thinking interpretation of the Bible.

In the *Tractatus politicus* he spoke up for democracy and pointed out the enormous importance of freedom of expression.

The *Ethica* (in full the *Ethica Ordine Geometrico Demonstrata*), Spinoza's masterwork, was meant to teach people how they could lessen their suffering. This was not philosophy for its own sake, because the book had a practical objective: to teach people to see that God is part of Creation, that everything that exists is a manifestation of God – including human beings. In order to come to this clear realisation it was of the utmost importance to be independent and free of intense passions. Spinoza lived his beliefs: his arguments were always presented calmly, were well-considered and reasonable. He did not ever allow himself to be provoked.

The *Ethica* appears to be structured like a geometric system. Spinoza uses definitions, axioms and propositions: in this way he tries to approach matters objectively despite the turbulence of the times. Throughout history many readers have complained that this makes the book very difficult to read. But then Spinoza has the last word, because the final sentence of the *Ethica* says: "All noble things are as difficult as they are rare."

5

References

Places to Go

Amsterdam: Amsterdam Esnoga (Portugese Synagogue)
Rijnsburg: Spinozahuis (Spinozahouse)
The Hague: Spinozahuis (Spinozahouse)
The Hague: Nieuwe Kerk (New Church: tomb of Spinoza)

Websites

www.britannica.com/EBchecked/topic/560202
www.philosophypages.com/ph/spin.htm

Captions

[page 54] *Portrait of Baruch de Spinoza,* Herzog August Bibliothek Wolfenbüttel/B 117
[left] Statue of Spinoza by Frédéric Hexamer, near his house in the Paviljoensgracht in The Hague
[right] The Spinozahouse in Rijnsburg and a Dutch banknote from 1972

ca. 1637 - 1863

Slavery

Human trafficking and forced labour in the New World

Since the great ocean crossing of Columbus in 1492, Europeans had been settling in what they called the New World, at the expense of the indigenous populations. The Portuguese began this by setting up sugar plantations in Brazil and having these worked by slaves brought across from Africa. This policy was adopted by all the European colonial powers. Together, in some two hundred years they transported over twelve million Africans in the transatlantic slave trade. The Dutch themselves transported more than 550,000 of these slaves. Some artists recorded their miserable lot in a drawing.

The Dutch slave trade started in 1621 with the establishment of the Dutch West India Company (WIC). WIC ships were originally sent out as privateers and to wage war on the Spanish-Portuguese fleet. In 1628, admiral Piet Hein captured the Spanish silver fleet, and in 1638 the Portuguese lost Saint George del Mina in modern-day Ghana to the WIC. In addition, parts of Brazil were occupied (1624-1654) and in 1665 the Republic's claim to colonial rights over the so-called Wild Coast (Surinam, Berbice, Essequibo-Demarary), and the Antillean islands of Aruba, Bonaire, Curaçao, Saint Martin, Saint Eustatius and Saba was recognised.

The Dutch became important players in the Atlantic area as a colonial power and slave traders. Up until 1730, the WIC held a monopoly on the slave trade. Subsequently, the Middelburg Commercial Company (established in 1720) grew into the biggest Dutch slave trader, with various auction houses in Rotterdam and Amsterdam to compete with the WIC. In around 1770, the Dutch slave trade reached its zenith, transporting some six thousand slaves each year. In following years these numbers quickly decreased.

Being a slave meant being forced to work and having no say in where, with whom and how you would live. The African slaves, and their descendants who were born into slavery, worked on plantations growing sugar, coffee, cocoa, cotton and tobacco. They worked in the salt ponds of Curaçao or waited on their masters.

Not all slaves accepted their lot. Particularly in Surinam, people escaped from slavery by running away. They settled in the jungle and established their own communities alongside those of the Indians. These fugitive slaves were referred to as Maroons or Bush Negroes. In addition, there were constant small and large slave uprisings on plantations and in the towns. The largest slave uprising took place on in 1795 on Curaçao under the leadership of Tula, who, inspired by the ideals of the French Revolution and the success of the slave uprising in Saint-Domingue (Haiti), demanded freedom. Tula, however, paid for his freedom with his life.

At the end of the eighteenth century, outrage against the slave trade was growing. This was true in the Netherlands too, even though discussions were often dominated by the interests of slave owners. Under pressure from the English, the slave trade was prohibited in 1814. In the Netherlands, the abolition of slave labour and slavery did not follow until 1 July 1863, making it one of the very last countries in Europe to emancipate its slaves.

57

References

Places to Go

Amsterdam and Middelburg: 'Slavernijroute'
(city walks on the subject of slavery)
Amsterdam: Nationaal instituut Nederlands
slavernijverleden en erfenis (Dutch National
Institute of Slavery and Heritage)
Amsterdam: Nationaal Scheepvaartmuseum Amsterdam
(National Maritime Museum Amsterdam)
Amsterdam, Oosterpark: Nationaal Slavernij Monument
(National Slavery Monument)
Amsterdam: Tropenmuseum
Rotterdam: Historisch Museum Rotterdam
(Historical Museum Rotterdam)
Rotterdam: Maritiem Museum Rotterdam
(Maritime Museum Rotterdam)
Vlissingen: Maritiem MuZEEum Vlissingen
(Maritime MuZEEum Vlissingen)

Websites

www.britannica.com/EBchecked/topic/174648
www.geheugenvannederland.nl
www.let.rug.nl/usa/E/newnetherlands/nl4.htm
(the Dutch West India Company in North America)
www.minbuza.nl/history/en/1600tot1700,
1600---1700.html
www.ninsee.nl
www.yale.edu/lawweb/avalon/westind.htm
(Charter of Privileges and Exemptions
of the Dutch West India Company)

Captions

[page 56 and above] Engravings from *Narrative of a Five Years' Expedition against the revolted Negroes of Surinam (1772 to 1777)*, John Gabriel Stedman, Collection of the Koninklijk Instituut voor de Tropen

Country mansions

Prosperous living in the countryside

Today, Goudestein mansion is the town hall of Maarssen, situated to the north of Utrecht on the River Vecht. For a long time it had been one of many country mansions along the river where wealthy residents of Amsterdam came to spend the summer.

If you take a trip on or alongside the Vecht, you will come across a great many country mansions, real palaces with magnificent gardens. This concentration along the river illustrates the immense wealth of Amsterdam in the Golden Age. Most of the mansions were built in the seventeenth century, some later. Wealthy merchants liked to escape the town in the summer months and enjoy the natural surroundings along the Vecht. Such escapes went hand in hand with large-scale relocations, usually by barge. The staff were moved as well as part of the household stocks – everyone and everything was brought along. The men

visited occasionally as they had to spend a lot of time working in town even over the summer months.

Goudestein is a textbook example of what happened to country mansions. In 1608, the Amsterdam merchant Jan Jacobszoon Huydekoper bought a large farmstead in Maarssen. His son Joan, a very important man in Amsterdam – he was, among other things, elected mayor on several occasions – subsequently had the Goudestein mansion built in 1628. In 1754 the seventeenth-century house was knocked down and replaced by the current palace. Up until the twentieth century the Huydekopers continued to live in the mansion. Then, in 1955, the municipality bought it and converted it into the town hall.

Influential people from Amsterdam invited many guests to their country retreats: friends from their social circles, as well as artists and intellectuals. The famous poet and scholar Constantijn

Huygens stayed at Goudestein in 1656 and apparently he enjoyed himself, for he wrote three spirited poems about the mansion.

The gardens of the houses were lovely and often still are today. They were inspired by the formal French style of landscaping, with tight geometric patterns. From this starting point, a new Dutch style evolved: ordered and geometric, but with baroque elements and playful additions like *theekoepels* (tea house gazebos), canals, water attractions and mazes. Needless to say, everyone wanted their garden to be a showpiece and each was more beautiful than the last.

The summer life in the country mansions of the aristocracy continued in the eighteenth century, although the economy in the Netherlands was slowing down. The wealthy families, however, were still able to live off their capital. Today, most of the country mansions are no longer owned by individuals. Instead they have become tourist attractions, prestigious business premises and venues for parties.

59

References

Places to Go
A visit to the country estates along the river Vecht, such as Gunterstein, Vreedenhoff and Bijdorp
A visit to similar country estates in the region of Kennemerland, such as Beeckestein
A boattrip along the river Vecht
Maarssen: Museum Maarssen

Websites
www.kasteleninutrecht.nl

Captions
[page 58] *Goudestein,* Municipality of Maarssen
[above] *Country mansion on the Vecht river,* Sijmen Hendriks/Hollandse Hoogte

1744 - 1828

Eise Eisinga

The Enlightenment in the Netherlands

Eise Eisinga was an amateur astronomer who built a planetarium in his own home in Franeker (Friesland). Today this planetarium is recognised as the oldest in the world.

The highly gifted Eisinga was not allowed to attend the Latin School because he was expected to become a woolcomber like his father before him. All on his own, he immersed himself in the study of the principles of maths and astronomy. The fact that the Franeker Academy was close by suited him well.

In 1774, a booklet was published in which it was forecast that the earth would be thrown out of its orbit by a collision between the moon and a number of other planets. This prediction caused a great deal of panic in Friesland. To demonstrate that there was no need for panic, Eisinga

decided to build a scale model of the solar system on the ceiling of his living room. In 1781 his planetarium was completed.

Just like many other men of his time, Eisinga was inspired by the Enlightenment. These men were convinced that knowledge could improve both mankind and society. Enlightenment thinkers in the Netherlands were different in nature to those in France. Living in a country with no all-powerful church or absolute ruler meant that few Dutch citizens were sympathetic to the radical and anti-clerical views of some French *philosophes*. Rather, they believed that God wanted the best for the world: He was leading all things towards a friendly, harmonious society. They therefore immersed themselves in enjoyable social interaction. Together with other responsible citizens, they conducted experiments in physics, they examined fossils, discussed solutions for social problems and studied heavenly bodies.

Even today, Eisinga's planetarium shows the current position of the planets, because the planets of the model take the same time to move around the sun as do the real planets: Mercury takes 88 days for its orbit, Earth 365 days and Saturn over 29 years. All this is kept in motion by an impressive gear mechanism of wooden rings and discs with ten thousand hand-forged nails as cog teeth. A pendulum clock and nine weights drive the gear mechanism.

When King William I came to Friesland in 1818 to visit the planetarium, he was so impressed that he subsequently bought it for the Dutch state. Ten years later, in 1828, Eisinga died aged 84. In his will he described the mechanism of his planetarium.

References

Places to Go

Amsterdam: New Metropolis Museum (NeMo)
Amsterdam: Planetarium Artis
Franeker: Koninklijk Eise Eisinga Planetarium
    (Royal Eise Eisinga Planetarium)
Haarlem: Teylers Museum
Leiden: Museum Boerhaave (Boerhaave Museum)

Websites

www.artis.nl/international/index.html
www.e-nemo.nl/en
www.museumboerhaave.nl/e_intro.html
www.omniversum.nl
www.planetarium-friesland.nl/engels.html
www.spaceexpo.nl
www.strw.leidenuniv.nl/index.php
www.teylersmuseum.nl

Captions

[page 60] *Ceiling of the planetarium,* Eise Eisinga
    Planetarium, Franeker
[left] *Portrait of Eisinga,* Willem Bartels van der Kooi,
    Eise Eisinga Planetarium, Franeker
[right] Interior of the planetarium and rad work above
    the planetarium, Eise Eisinga Planetarium, Franeker

1780 - 1795

The patriots

Political conflict about modernising the Republic

By the second half of the eighteenth century, the Golden Age of the Republic definitely seemed to be over. As a trading nation, the Republic had been surpassed by England. Although the financial sector was growing, it was unable to cope with increasing unemployment. The voice of the Republic was barely listened to in international politics. This was made painfully clear in the Fourth Anglo-Dutch War (1780-1784), in which the Republic could offer little resistance to the English.

A new political group came to the fore during this crisis. Citizens who up until then had had almost no say in the administration of the towns and the country itself. They regarded Stadholder (governor) William V as a kind of dictator and the ruling class as his puppets. They held the Stadholder responsible for the crisis in which the country found itself. These critical citizens called themselves the *Patriots*. Some members of the ruling class sided with the patriots.

On 26 September 1781, an anonymous, illegal patriot pamphlet was published, addressed "To the people of the Netherlands". It had an explosive effect on the political discussions. Two parties became clearly defined: the supporters of Stadholder William V, and, on the other side, the patriots. Both sides made full use of political pamphlets. The country was inundated by an avalanche of magazines – such as the influential *De Kruyer* – single-page flyers and cartoons. All of these analysed how the Republic was organised and why it was failing, and put forward solutions. Gradually, new elements were brought into the discussions. This was the start of a national feeling, pride in one's own country, a feeling that began to play an increasingly larger role. People no longer simply thought of themselves as inhabitants of a town or region, but also as citizens of the fatherland, which, according to the patriots, should therefore be organised as a political unity.

One moot point in this issue was how the citizens would be represented politically.

Patriot citizens organised themselves into 'vrijkorpsen', volunteer corps, a kind of militia to take over the country. Stadholder William V no longer felt safe in the patriot town of The Hague and he retreated to Nijmegen until the Prussian king sent in troops in 1787 to restore order.

The Prussian king's sister, Wilhelmina (wife of the Stadholder) had requested him to take this action. The patriot militia could not stand up to the well-trained Prussian soldiers. Eight years later (in 1795) the Republic came to its end after all, when the revolutionary French came to the aid of the (underground) patriots to overthrow the old regime.

References

Places to Go

Amsterdam: Amsterdams Historisch Museum
  (Amsterdam Historical Museum)
Dordrecht: Simon van Gijn – museum aan huis
  (museum at home)

Websites

www.britannica.com/EBchecked/topic/446697
www.britannica.com/EBchecked/topic/644197
www.minbuza.nl/history/en/oorlog,1781.html
www.simonvangijn.nl/

Captions

[page 62] Engraving from *De politieke kruyer*,
  Universiteitsbibliotheek UvA, Special Collections
[above] Coloured engraving entitled: *Princess Wilhelmina held captive*, G.A. Lehman, Atlas van Stolk, Rotterdam

1769 - 1821

Napoleon Bonaparte
The French period

The history of the Netherlands can never truly be separated from developments outside the country. This certainly applies to the end of the eighteenth century and the beginning of the nineteenth century, when the French exerted decisive influence on Dutch politics and the "little corporal" Napoleon Bonaparte was France's leader. Napoleon was a military man who overthrew the French government in 1799 and afterwards took control not only of France but also of all the territories conquered by French armies. Subsequently, as a general, he led his troops in battle against the Emperor of Austria, the Tsar of Russia and the King of England.

From 1806, Emperor Napoleon ruled almost the whole of Europe as an "enlightened despot".

The Dutch Republic had already fallen to French troops in 1795 with the aid of Dutch patriots. Until 1806, the Batavian Republic, as the Netherlands was then known, remained officially independent of France but in actuality little took place without the approval of the French.

In 1806, Napoleon appointed his brother Louis as King of Holland, and the Netherlands became a kingdom. This laid the foundations for the later monarchy.

In 1810 Napoleon deposed his brother and the Netherlands was absorbed into the French Empire. Three years later, Napoleon was defeated and banished to Elba; the Netherlands regained its independence.

Napoleon clearly played a leading role in the history of Europe at this time. One of his major achievements was that he modernised administration procedures and justice systems in the areas he controlled. He also implemented new weights (the kilogramme) and measurements (the metre). In addition, the registry of births, deaths and marriages was introduced whereby everyone had to adopt a surname.

The Dutch response to these modernisations was divided. For example, some believed that the *Code Napoleon*, the French civil code, was an enormous improvement compared to their own local laws. The new civil code created a rule of law under which everyone was equal, and in which the dispensation of justice was public. Its opponents felt that Napoleon had not taken into consideration the greatly varying local customs and arrangements. The introduction of conscription met with just as much resistance, especially when the demand for soldiers for the seemingly never-ending wars continued to grow.

After the fall of Napoleon no one thought about reversing the Napoleonic innovations. The *Code Napoleon* therefore remained in force, just like many more of Napoleon's innovations.

References

Places to Go

Amsterdam: Koninklijk Paleis op de Dam
   (City Hall/Royal Palace Amsterdam)
Amsterdam: Trippenhuis (Trippen House; home to the
   Royal Institute of Sciences, Literature and Fine Arts
   founded by King Louis Napoleon, nowadays the
   Royal Netherlands Academy of Arts and Sciences)
Delft: Legermuseum (Army Museum)
Haarlem: Provinciehuis van Noord-Holland
   (Province House of North Holland; Haarlem
   residence of King Louis Napoleon)
Woudenberg: Pyramide van Austerlitz
   (Pyramid of Austerlitz)

Websites

www.britannica.com/EBchecked/topic/55774
www.britannica.com/EBchecked/topic/72710
www.britannica.com/EBchecked/topic/402943
www.knaw.nl/organisatie/trippenhuis/
   historie_huis.html
www.minbuza.nl/history/en/oorlog,1793.html
www.minbuza.nl/history/en/oorlog,
   1806-1810.html

Captions

[page 64] *Etude de Tête pour un portrait de Napoléon Ier en costume de Sacre,* David Jacques Louis, Photo RMN/Christian Jean/89-002118/T184
[above] *Portrait of Napoleon on the Imperial Throne,* Jean-Auguste-Dominique Ingres, Musée de l'Armée, Paris

1772 - 1843

King William I

The kingdom of the Netherlands and Belgium

In 1813, after the end of French rule, the son of Stadholder William V returned to the Netherlands to accept the crown. This was a clear break with tradition. Unlike his father, William I did not become Stadholder (governor) of all the provinces but rather king of a unified state in which he played the main political role.

In 1815, the so-called Austrian Low Countries (modern-day Belgium) were united with the territory of the former Republic to serve as a buffer against the defeated French. And so, the United Kingdom of the Netherlands was created. In European terms it was a medium-sized country controlling large colonial territories. The energetic William (whose nickname was "king-merchant") tried to restore the previously thriving economy by stimulating its strengths in the three parts of the country (the north, south and the Indies). The south, where an Industrial Revolution had taken place early, had to concentrate on producing consumer goods. The traders in the north subsequently had to transport these goods across the world. And finally, the inhabitants of the colonies were to supply valuable tropical goods. The King had canals dug and roads laid between the north and south to make transport more easy. He himself acted as an investor. In 1824, William set up the Netherlands Trading Company for trade with the Dutch East Indies. The "cultivation system" or "culture system" was introduced in the East Indies, under which the indigenous population was obliged to work for the colonial authorities on the land for a period of each year. The products were sold by the Netherlands Trading Company.

Despite his economic endeavours, the King was not popular among the Belgians. Belgian liberals saw him as a ruler who desired absolute power and who was not prepared to tolerate any increased participation on the part of the educated elite. Belgian Catholics objected to the interference of the Protestant king in the training of novice priests. In 1830, the citizens of Brussels rebelled. They were inspired by the aria "*Amour sacrée de la patrie*" that had been sung in their theatre. William I sent an army against them but to no avail. Belgium was granted independence. Nevertheless, William I kept the army called up for nine years – incurring extremely high costs – something that damaged his reputation in the Netherlands very badly. In 1839 he finally recognised Belgium's independence. In the following year, a disillusioned William I abdicated from the throne.

References

Places to Go
Amsterdam: Amsterdams Historisch Museum
   (Amsterdam Historical Museum)
Amsterdam: Koninklijk Paleis op de Dam
   (City Hall/Royal Palace)
Delft: Nieuwe Kerk (New Church:
   William I was buried in the Royal Crypt)
Frederiksoord (agricultural colony, established
   in 1818 by the Society of Charity which was
   inspired by William I)

Websites
www.ahm.nl
www.britannica.com/EBchecked/topic/644033/William-I
www.koninklijkhuis.nl
www.minbuza.nl/history/en/1813tot1914,1813.html
www.minbuza.nl/history/en/1813tot1914,1830.html

Captions
[page 66] *William I with a map of Java,* Joseph Paelinck,
   Collection of the Rijksmuseum Amsterdam/SK-C-1460
[above] *Tableau of the September days in 1830,
   Grote Markt,* Egide Charles Gustave Wappers,
   Musée d'Art Ancien, Brussels

1839
The first railway
Acceleration

On 20 September 1839, the first railway line in the Netherlands was opened with a festive celebration. The steam locomotive "*De Arend*" took twenty-five minutes to travel from Amsterdam to Haarlem. A lot of people were not impressed: the train went too fast and made much too much noise. Was this novelty really necessary and was it safe? Near Ghent at the beginning of the same year, the steam boiler of a departing train had exploded. This innovation was doomed to failure and after all, barges were a fine mode of transport, weren't they?

Despite all the initial scepticism, the first train heralded a time of enormous change. The Amsterdam-Haarlem line was quickly extended into what became known as the "*Old Line*" running from Amsterdam to Rotterdam. Work on the second major rail link began in 1843, connecting Amsterdam with Utrecht. More lines followed, all run by different railway operators. By about 1900, the train had become the most important mode of transport in the Netherlands.

Today, it is hard to imagine the enormous changes the railways brought about in Dutch society. Before the arrival of the railways, travelling cost a great deal of time. It was too expensive for most people and was sometimes dangerous. In terms of travelling time, the railways made the Netherlands much smaller. The improved links and travel comfort contributed greatly to the unification of the country: people from different regions came into contact with one another more often and the state was able to better organise its national territory.

The railway network was a pre-condition for the industrialisation of the Netherlands, which only really took off after 1870. Raw materials, products and workers too all had to be transported. In its turn, industrialisation contributed to the further expansion of the railway network. At the beginning of the twentieth century, the Netherlands had a dense railway network. In the thirties, however, many lines were closed – particularly local ones. In 1938, all the lines were incorporated into one nationalised company: NV Nederlandse Spoorwegen (NS) that continued to exist until the reorganisation of 1995. The state and all kinds of lobby organisations are still actively involved in the now privatised NS and its services. This indicates that railways have remained a vital component of Dutch society.

References

Places to Go

Apeldoorn-Dieren/Goes-Borsele/Simpelveld-Schin
op Geul: Take a ride on a steam train on one of
these tracks.
Brussels: Museum van de Belgische Spoorwegen
(Belgian Railway Museum)
Utrecht: Spoorwegmuseum (Railway Museum)
Rotterdam: Museum van de Stoom Stichting Nederland
(Museum of the Dutch Steam Foundation)

Websites

www.spoorwegmuseum.nl/en
www.stoomstichting.nl

Captions

[page 68] *The "Arend" powered by steam,*
Collection of the Spoorwegmuseum
[above] *Opening of the first Amsterdam-Haarlem link,*
Collection of the Spoorwegmuseum

1848

The Constitution

Fundamental rules and principles of government

The Constitution is the most important law of a state. (The word "state" refers to an autonomous territory in which power is exercised over the inhabitants.) The Constitution determines who exercises power in practice in such a state and how this will take place. The Dutch Constitution sets out, for example, the role of the monarch and that of the ministers. The Constitution also states how other laws are to be made, what duties judges have and what the tasks of the municipalities and provinces are. Moreover, the Constitution sets out what influence and power Dutch citizens have in the state.

Right at the beginning, the Dutch Constitution sets out the rights of citizens in terms of the state: basic rights. Basic rights are not the rights of citizens amongst one another but rather the rights of citizens to live their own lives without the interference of the state in their opinions and life choices.

The first article of the Constitution promises that all people, no matter

how different they are or what different opinions they hold, will be treated equally by the state. In the articles that follow, the Constitution states, among other things, that citizens have the right to practice their own religion, the right to exchange ideas with one another; and the right to express their opinions in public.

The state can only restrict such rights – like freedom of worship and freedom of speech – if it is absolutely necessary. For example, someone's freedom may be restricted if that person presents a danger to others. In such instances the state may act, but only in accordance with the law.

No Constitution existed in the Netherlands in the Middle Ages. The ruler had the power and did not have to conform to the law. In later times, some groups of people did gain rights in respect of their ruler, but it was only from the eighteenth century onwards that everyone had rights and that every institution entitled to exercise power was obliged to obey the law. This was set down in a Constitution in the

Netherlands in 1798. The "Constitution of the Kingdom of the Netherlands" that still applies today was drafted in 1815.

It is easier to change other laws than it is to change the Constitution. However, significant amendments to the Constitution have been made. In 1848 King William II agreed to amend the Constitution so that the monarch would have less power and the people more. This amendment was so dramatic that the "Constitution of 1848", drafted by constitutional law expert Thorbecke, is regarded as the beginning of democracy in the Netherlands. Nonetheless, it was only in 1917 that the right to vote was extended to include all men. Women were granted the passive right to vote at the same time. In 1922, the active right to vote for women – that was introduced in 1919 – was finally set down in the Constitution.

71

```
 O P G E S O M D   Z O N D E R
E I G E N D O M   G E B O O R T E
O E   I E M A N D   B E H O O R T
T A A T   ■   E E N   I E D E R
A N D E L   I N   I E D E R E   V
D E R   H E E F T   W A A R   H I
I J K E   B E S C H E R M I N G
E N   D E R G E L I J K E   A C H
I J N   M E T   D E   G R O N D R
O L L E   G E L I J K H E I D   R
I J N   R E C H T   N   E N   V E
V E R V O L G D   E E F T   E R
B O R G E N   N   I G   V O O R
I G   V E R Z U   W E L K E
E V E N M I N   L   E E N   Z
N   W I L L E   U R I G E   I N
T E G E N   E N   E R G E L I
```

References

Places to Go

Locally: a visit to a Dutch court of law or a local council
The Hague: a visit to the Tweede Kamer der Staten-Generaal, the Dutch House of Representatives

Websites

www.britannica.com/EBchecked/topic/409956/The-Netherlands
www.inghist.nl/Onderzoek/Projecten/Grondwet/index_html_en
www.minbuza.nl/history/en/1813tot1914,1848.html
www.tweedekamer.nl

Captions

[page 70] *The Constitution of 1848,* Beeldbank Nationaal Archief
[above] *Portrait of Johan Rudolf Thorbecke,* Johan Heinrich Neuman, Collection of the Rijksmuseum Amsterdam/SK-A-4120
[left] *The text of the Dutch Constitution on a wall in The Hague,* Jan Kooi

1860

Max Havelaar

Scandal in the East Indies

In 1859 Eduard Douwes Dekker, a disappointed civil servant in the Dutch East Indies, wrote a book under the pseudonym "Multatuli". This book was entitled "Max Havelaar or the Coffee Auctions of the Dutch Trading Company". It was a condemnation of the abuses of the Dutch colonial administration in the Dutch East Indies.

The book is a frame story with various interwoven storylines. It begins with the tale of Batavus Droogstoppel, a coffee broker and textbook example of a petty bourgeois, unimaginative, miserly man who symbolises how the Netherlands was profiting from its colonies in the East Indies. On a certain day, a former classmate (Sjaalman) visits Droogstoppel and asks him to publish a manuscript.

What follows – interrupted by Droogstoppel's commentary – is the tale

of the manuscript that relates in broad lines the actual experiences of Multatuli (alias Max Havelaar) as assistant-resident in the Dutch East Indies. (This is largely history as experienced by the writer Eduard Douwes Dekker himself as a civil servant.) Assistant-resident Havelaar takes up the cause of the oppressed islanders, the Javanese, but his Dutch superiors and local profiteers who do business with the Dutch work against him.

A number of native stories are woven into the book, for example, the story of Saidjah and Adinda. Between the lines of this moving love story lies a bitter indictment of the exploitation and cruelties to which the native Javanese were subjected. At the end of the book, Multatuli addresses a passionate plea directly to King William III, who, as head of state, was ultimately responsible for the abuses and corruption of the administration in the Dutch East Indies.

Initially, the book received a lot of criticism, but it quickly created a storm and was reprinted many times. It is still in print today and has been translated into over 140 languages. In 1999, the Indonesian writer Pramoedya Ananta Toer referred to the book in The New York Times as "The Book That Killed Colonialism".

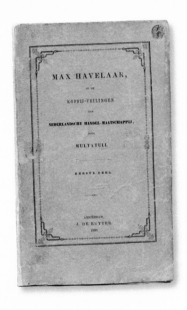

References

Places to Go

Amsterdam: Multatuli Museum
Amsterdam: Statue of Multatuli at the Torensluis
　　Bridge across the Singel
Amsterdam: Tropenmuseum
Delft: Museum Nusantara (museum about
　　the history and cultures of Indonesia)

Websites

www.britannica.com/EBchecked/topic/370353
www.britannica.com/EBchecked/topic/396970/Multatuli
www.geheugenvannederland.nl
www.multatuli-museum.nl/en
www.textual.net/access.gutenberg?author=Multatuli&site
www.tropenmuseum.nl
www.ucl.ac.uk/dutch/self_study_packs/english_
　　language/multatuli/index.html

Captions

[page 72] *Cover of Max Havelaar*, published by Pandora
[left] *First edition of Max Havelaar*
[right] *Drawing of Multatuli*, August Allebé,
　　Collection of the Multatuli Museum
[beneath] Statue of Multatuli by Hans Bayens

Opposition to child labour

Out of the workplace and back to school

Child labour was a normal and usual occurrence in the nineteenth century. Children worked on the land and in shops or workshops. This was considered very sensible – they could learn a trade in this way – but often it was necessary for children to work to supplement the family income. When, during the Industrial Revolution, children were put to work in factories as well, more and more objections were raised against child labour – at least in factories.

Working conditions in factories were usually very poor. A well-known story is that of Petrus Regout's glass factory in Maastricht, where the kilns burned day and night. The factory had two shifts of workers, each working twelve hours at a stretch. Half-asleep, children aged between eight and ten years old would have to walk to work at about midnight to start their shift. Regout saw no problem in this. He believed that children could do with less sleep.

In about 1860, criticism of child labour became more intense. Doctors and teachers explained that working was unhealthy and that the proper place for children was at school. Factory operators began to realise that children would be better off starting work once they had completed their primary education. Moreover, children aged twelve years and older who could read and write could be put to better use in the factories. At the same time, the need for child labour decreased as increasingly more work was done by machines. The attitude of parents also began to change with the times. As their wages began to rise and the need to supplement their income with their children's wages became less pressing, parents started to send their children to school more often and for longer periods of time.

Two Acts contributed to this development. The *Kinderwet van Van Houten* (the Child Labour Act of 1874) prohibited children under the age of twelve from working in workshops and factories. This did not mean, however, that child labour in factories was fully abolished with immediate effect. Furthermore, children were not prohibited from doing farm work. The *Leerplichtwet* (Compulsory Education Act of 1900) put an end to child labour once and for all. From that time onwards, parents were obliged to send children aged between seven and twelve years old to school. In practice, most parents were already doing so. By about 1900, ninety percent of all children were attending school.

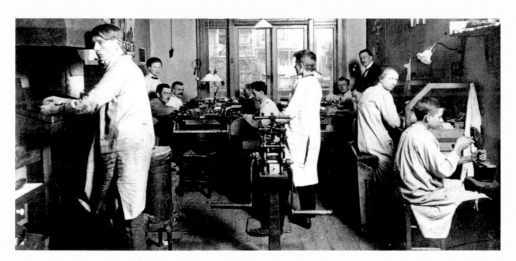

1874 No. 27.

DE EERSTE WET, TE DANKEN AAN HET INITIATIEF DER TWEEDE KAMER.

De fabriekskinderen: »Leve mijnheer van Houten!"

References

Places to Go
Arnhem: Openluchtmuseum (Open-air Museum)
Leiden: Stedelijk Museum De Lakenhal
      (City Museum The Lakenhal)
Ootmarsum: Openluchtmuseum (Open-air Museum)
Rotterdam: Nationaal Onderwijsmuseum
      (National Museum of Education)
Tilburg: Audax Textielmuseum Tilburg
      (Audax Textile Museum Tilburg)

Websites
www.britannica.com/EBchecked/topic/111059/
      child-labour
www.lakenhal.nl/en/index.html

Captions
[page 74] *Sewing burlap sacks*,
      Beeldbank Nationaal Archief/BG A23/648
[above] *Child labour in the printing industry*,
      Beeldbank Nationaal Archief BG B15/237
[left] *The children of the factory: "Long live Sir
      Van Houten"*, Elias Spanier, Rijksmuseum,
      inv. nr. RP-P-OB-76.771

1853 - 1890

Vincent van Gogh
The modern artist

Every year, some one and a half million people visit the Van Gogh Museum in Amsterdam. Eighty to ninety percent of these visitors come from outside the Netherlands. The Dutch painter Vincent van Gogh is famous in all four corners of the globe.

This was not the case in the nineteenth century during his lifetime. Van Gogh had a difficult life filled with upheaval, lost loves and financial problems. Despair ultimately drove him to commit suicide. Only after his death did his star begin to rise. On the one hand, this was because of his paintings: powerful images, with vibrant colours, different. Many people of all ages appreciate his work. On the other hand, people are interested in Van Gogh's life story. His is the textbook tale of the artist whose genius is only matched by his loneliness.

Van Gogh was born in 1853 in the village of Zundert in the province of Brabant. At a young age he travelled across the Netherlands and Europe. In 1885, in Nuenen, he painted the famous picture "The Potato Eaters", a dark portrait of a peasant family. The following year he went to Paris. Van Gogh's brother Theo, an art dealer in Paris, showed him paintings and drawings of the Impressionists, artists whose use of colour and light was more refined than what Vincent was used to. Vincent was also impressed by the Japanese prints he viewed.

In 1888, he rented a studio in the south of France: the "Yellow House" in Arles. He wrote to his younger sister Wil that the lavish natural beauty of the south demanded a new way of painting: "Distinctly colourful: sky blue, pink, orange, vermillion, bright yellow, bright green, bright wine-red, violet". Vincent painted landscapes and, because he could not afford to pay for models, many self-portraits.

The French artist Paul Gauguin came to stay with Vincent, but they had an argument. Van Gogh became so confused that he threatened Gauguin with a razor. Shortly afterwards Van Gogh cut of a portion of his left ear, either accidentally or on purpose. Some of his self-portraits show him with his ear bandaged.

Van Gogh became increasingly neurotic and had himself committed to a psychiatric institution where he painted his famous cypresses and starry skies. On 27 July 1890 he walked into a corn field and shot himself in the chest. He died two days later.

Today, Vincent van Gogh is such a highly appreciated artist that his work hangs in museums throughout the world and is worth huge amounts of money. His portrait of the owner of the café in Arles, "*L'Arlésienne*", was auctioned in New York in 2006 for 40.3 million dollars (33.9 million euros). That is the equivalent of the price of a Boeing 737 commercial airliner.

77

References

Places to Go
Amsterdam: Van Gogh Museum
Nuenen: Van Gogh Documentatiecentrum
    (Van Gogh Documentation Centre)
Otterlo: Museum Kröller-Müller
Zundert: Van Goghhuis (Van Gogh House),
    Van Gogh bicycle and walking route

Websites
www.britannica.com/EBchecked/topic/237118
www.kmm.nl
www.tefaf.com
www.vangoghmuseum.nl
www.vggallery.com

Captions
[page 76] *Sunflowers,* Vincent van Gogh, 1888,
    Van Gogh Museum (Vincent van Gogh Stichting)
[left] *Self Portrait,* Vincent van Gogh, 1887,
    Van Gogh Museum (Vincent van Gogh Stichting)
[right] Vincent van Gogh, 1873

1854 - 1929

Aletta Jacobs

The emancipation of women

Aletta Jacobs was the first woman in Dutch history to be officially admitted to university. This took place in 1871. As a schoolgirl she had written a letter to Prime Minister Thorbecke requesting permission to be allowed to attend "academic classes". Aletta Jacobs' dream was to become a doctor. Thorbecke answered within a week, but did not write to Aletta herself. Instead, he wrote to her father that permission had been granted. And so, thanks to a seventeen-year-old girl, in 1871 universities in the Netherlands were opened to women. Prior to this time, universities and most schools as well were only open to young men. Only Anna

Maria van Schurman, an educated woman (she had a command of no less than ten languages) who lived in the seventeenth century, had ever been allowed to attend any lectures (in Utrecht). However, she had had to sit behind a curtain so as not to cause a distraction for the young men.

Throughout her life, Aletta Jacobs fought for the rights of women. As a doctor, for example, she opened a practice that assisted women with contraception so that they did not have to become pregnant every year. She also fought against the abuses of the retail trade. In her practice in Amsterdam, she had noticed that shop girls suffered from many physical complaints because they were forced to remain standing for the entire working day (which was then eleven hours long). Thanks to Aletta Jacobs, a bill was passed that obliged shops to provide their staff with seating facilities. For fifty years, Aletta Jacobs also fought for the right to vote for women, together with other men and women who supported the rights of women. These women called themselves "feminists" and made their voices heard in a variety of ways: they organised exhibitions, published newspapers and pamphlets, established societies, held demonstrations and submitted petitions. However, it was only in 1919 that the right to vote for women was introduced in the Dutch Constitution. In 1922, Dutch women voted for the first time. Aletta Jacobs was 68 years old at the time.

For centuries, politics had been the exclusive domain of men, just like the academic world, the Church and the armed forces. People believed that women were not the equals of men: their job was to run the household and care for children, and therefore they could not participate in public life. There had always been criticism of this "patriarchal" view of life, but real changes only took place in the twentieth century. And a second wave of feminist campaigning was needed to achieve these changes. In the early 1970s, the *"dolle minas"* [Dutch women's libbers] carried out a campaign for the emancipation of women. They did not want to be condemned to lives as housewives like their mothers before them. In 1980 the Equal Opportunities Act came into force.

References

Places to Go
Groningen: Universiteitsmuseum (University Museum)
Heesch: Poppenhuismuseum (Doll's House Museum)

Websites
www.alettajacobs.org/english
www.inghist.nl/Onderzoek/Projecten/DVN/en/
www.iiav.nl
www.rug.nl/genderstudies/universiteit/alettajacobs
www.vrouwengeschiedenis.dds.nl

Captions
[page 78] *Aletta as a new graduate of medicine,* Bibliotheek der Rijksuniversiteit Groningen
[above] SDAP demonstration for universal suffrage in Amsterdam, 1916

1914 - 1918

World War I

War and neutrality

From 1914 to 1918 the "Great War" raged in Europe. The war did have consequences for the Netherlands, but the country was spared its horrors. In World War I, the Central Powers (Germany, Austria and Turkey) were opposed by the Allies (France, Great Britain and Russia). However, what it actually came down to was the soldiers of the two sides facing one another along kilometres of trenches. When shooting broke out, the soldiers could do little else than take cover from the exploding shells and hope for the best. They were even more powerless when they had to attack the enemy. As soon as they went over the top of the trenches, they were mowed down by the machine guns of the other side. The use of poison gas was something new in this war. Ultimately the war cost millions of lives.

When the United States joined the Allies in 1917, the balance was tipped in the Allies' favour. In November of the following year the Central Powers surrendered.

During the war, the Netherlands had remained neutral, something that had been a principle of Dutch foreign politics for some time. The Dutch army was, however, mobilised to defend its own territory. Furthermore, the Netherlands had to deal with the peripheral effects of the war. Large numbers of Belgian refugees had to be taken in, in temporary camps, among other places. Unemployment rose due to the fall in international trade and the sinking (by torpedoes) of many merchant vessels. Food became scarce and rationing was introduced. In 1917 and 1918, despairing housewives plundered food stocks in Amsterdam and Rotterdam.

Many European countries experienced the upheaval of revolution during or after the war. In Russia, the Tsar was forced from the throne and executed, and the German and Austro-Hungarian empires were replaced by republics. In the Netherlands, radical political changes were implemented during the war. In 1917 all men were granted the right to vote. After the war, in 1919, this was followed by universal suffrage for women. From 1919 onwards, the Netherlands was a fully democratic country: every adult man and woman had the right to vote in elections.

References

Places to Go

Alkmaar: Le Poilu (First World War Museum)
Delft: Legermuseum (Army Museum, trench art)
The city of Ieper and surroundings, where heavy fights took place during the First World War
Ieper (Belgium): In Flanders Fields Museum
Ieper (Belgium): Ramparts War Museum

Websites

www.britannica.com/EBchecked/topic/648646/World-War-I
www.minbuza.nl/history/en/1914tot1966, 1914---1918.html
www.wereldoorlog1418.nl/refugees

Captions

[page 80] *Australian soldiers with gas masks* (1917), Imperial War Museum/Captain Frank Hurley
[top left] *Man holding a heavy loaded bicycle in balance, two children and a large bundle of clothing on it, Refugees from Belgium* (1914), Nationaal Archief
[top right] *Red Cross transporting wounded soldiers in Rotterdam* (1914), Nationaal Archief
[beneath left] *Arrival of Belgian refugees on a horse-drawn cart from the port of Antwerp*, Regionaal Historisch Centrum Bergen op Zoom
[beneath right] *Western front, Belgian and French soldiers in a trench* (1917), unknown

1917 - 1931

De Stijl

Revolution in design

Gerrit Rietveld's famous red and blue chair of 1918 is not only red and blue: the frame is yellow and black.

The chair therefore still meets the requirements that the artists of the *De Stijl* (The Style) movement upheld with regard to visual arts. In their eyes, only the three primary colours (red, blue and yellow) and the three "non-colours" (black, white and grey) were acceptable. Moreover, all lines had to be straight and the angles right-angles.

Their principles of colour are still reflected, for example, in the works of Dick Bruna ("Miffy"). In fact, Dick Bruna was influenced by De Stijl but he deviated from the strict principles by immediately using the colour green and curved lines. More important than the design aspects of De Stijl was the substantive task that the artists set themselves. The artistic content of their work was not meant to

reflect reality, but rather to express the harmony that they believed was the law of the universe. This harmony demanded abstract shapes – straight lines and bright colours. Their works of art therefore did not simply reflect the incidental state of mind of the artist but helped the public along the path to truth and purity.

The group and their monthly journal called "*De Stijl*" were established in 1917. It is easy to understand that this longing for harmony developed in the chaotic times of the World War I. The journal continued to be printed until 1931, when the artist Theo van Doesburg died. After his death the group dissolved. The artists who made up *De Stijl* were not a fixed group: the composition fluctuated. The architect Gerrit Rietveld and the artist Piet Mondrian, two of the move-ment's key members, never even met one another.

De Stijl was very internationally-oriented and gained an international reputation. And yet the movement was firmly rooted in Dutch traditions. The art historian H.L.C. Jaffé once said that the aim of De Stijl – to achieve the abstract, beauty and purity – had its origins in the iconoclasm and the restrained, Calvinist art of seventeenth-century Dutch painters like Vermeer, Saenredam and De Hooch.

According to Jaffé, one can even see similarities between the art of De Stijl and the struggle of the Dutch to master nature. After all, the Dutch landscape with its precise geometric shapes, its straight lines and waterways brings to mind the paintings of Mondrian. In short, geometry and precision, the abstract and purity had been sought in the Netherlands for centuries and this is reflected in the artistic works of the De Stijl movement.

References

Places to Go

Amsterdam: Stedelijk Museum (City Museum)
Utrecht: Centraal Museum (Central Museum)
Utrecht: Schröderhuis
    (Schröderhouse: design by Gerrit Rietveld)
Rotterdam: Café De Unie (design by J.J.P. Oud)
The Hague: Gemeentemuseum (Municipal Museum)

Websites

www.britannica.com/EBchecked/topic/566242/De-Stij
www.centraalmuseum.nl
www.gemeentemuseum.nl
www.kmm.nl
www.rietveldschroderhuis.nl
www.stedelijk.nl

Captions

[page 82] Red and blue armchair, Gerrit Rietveld, Collection of the Centraal Museum, Utrecht
[left] Composition in Red, Blue and Yellow (1930), Piet Mondrian, Fukuoka City Bank LTD, Fukuoka, Japan
[right] Rietveldt-Schröderhuis, Collection of the Centraal Museum, Utrecht

1929 - 1940

The crisis years

Society in the depression

The years from 1929 to 1940 are usual referred to as the "crisis years" or the "great depression": a long period of a falling economy and large-scale unemployment. The crisis began in October 1929 in the United States after the Wall Street Crash and soon the whole world was in the grip of the depression.

The number of unemployed in the Netherlands in 1930 totalled about 100,000 and reached its peak in 1936 with 480,000 people out of work. The numbers fell somewhat after this time but until the outbreak of the war, hundreds of thousands of people remained out of work. Up until then, unemployment rates in the Netherlands had never been this high and the situation had never lasted for so long. One out of every four Dutch citizens had been out of work for a year or longer.

The government decided to provide the unemployed with financial support.

This support could not be too high, because – according to the government – that would make the unemployed lazy. The benefit paid out was just enough to pay the rent and provide a simple meal. There was no money left for entertainment, sports or clothes. To prevent the unemployed from accepting cash-in-hand work alongside their benefit, they had to have their dole card stamped at unemployment office once or twice a day. This was considered very humiliating. In addition, the unemployed could be forced to work in the relief work programme. This meant that a teacher could be forced to take a spade and dig ditches or build dykes. Large public works like the *Amsterdamse Bos* (Amsterdam Woods) date from this time.

The government, under Prime Minister Colijn, chose to keep its hands on the purse strings as much as possible.

The budget had to be balanced, and for a long time Colijn refused to reconsider the value of the Dutch guilder. This policy of economising was highly criticised – particularly by the socialists who believed that the government needed to implement a much stronger economic policy.

The government appeared powerless to resolve the crisis and many Dutch citizens began to have doubts about their parliamentary democracy: the system seemed to represent division and lack of decisive action. This criticism did not, however, lead to a significant shift of votes to the right or left at the elections. The large democratic parties managed to retain most of their support. The National Socialist Movement, which promoted powerful leadership, remained a small right-wing party with little support.

After World War II, new ideas arose about tackling the problem of unemployment. Unemployed people were approached in a more human, less suspicious manner. In addition, the government made greater efforts to assist the unemployed in finding work.

References

Places to Go
Amsterdam: Amsterdams Historisch Museum
(Amsterdam Historical Museum)
Amsterdam: bezoekerscentrum Amsterdamse Bos
(Visitor Information Centre of the Amsterdam wood)
Amsterdam: Vakbondsmuseum De Burcht
(Unionmuseum The Burcht)

Websites
www.britannica.com/EBchecked/topic/243118
www.iisg.nl (This is the website of one of the world's largest documentary and research institutions in the field of social history in general and the history of the labour movement in particular)
www.minbuza.nl/history/en/1914tot1966,1929.html

Captions
[page 84] *"Who will help me along"*, Spaarnestad Photo
[above] *Unemployed men lined up*, Spaarnestad Photo
[right] *Prime Minister Hendrik Colijn during a speech*
(1938), ANP Historisch Archief

1940 - 1945

World War II

Occupation and liberation

In 1933 Adolf Hitler came to power in Germany. He was the leader of the National Socialist German Workers Party, the NSDAP, known in English as the Nazi Party which promoted anti-Semitism. The party profited from the discontent felt by many Germans about the humiliating way in which Germany had been treated after World War I. Hitler intended to make Germany the most powerful country in Europe. He first directed attacks on Austria, Czechoslovakia and Poland. Subsequently he planned to neutralise Germany's most stringent opponent in Western Europe: France. Both the Netherlands and Belgium were to be occupied in Hitler's invasion of France.

On the morning of Friday, 10 May 1940, many Dutch citizens were awoken by the droning of aircraft, exploding bombs and the rattling of tanks. German soldiers had crossed the border. The war had started. The Dutch army was far too weak to stand up to the force of the German assault. Once the Germans had bombed the centre of Rotterdam into the ground and were threatening to treat other cities in the same way, the Dutch military command decided to surrender. The government and the queen had already fled to England.

Initially, the occupation did not seem too bad, but it quickly became clear what occupation really meant. Dutch men were forced to go and work in German factories. People were also taken away to prisons and concentration camps without any form of due process. The Jews in particular were persecuted. The occupying Germans transported over 100,000 Jewish men, women and children in freight trains from the Netherlands to concentration camps where most of them were put to death.

The Germans were assisted by members of the Dutch National Socialist Movement (NSB), who had a similar ideology, and by hangers-on and profiteers. On the other side was the resistance movement, which gained a lot of support towards the end of the war in particular. The great majority of the Dutch population was anti-German but passive.

In the autumn of 1944, the south of the country was liberated by allied troops. The area above the great rivers, however (particularly the towns in the western provinces), had to endure the "winter of starvation" before being liberated in their turn. An extreme food shortage weakened the population and tens of thousands died. In May 1945 the German commander signed the surrender and the whole of the Netherlands was liberated. At that time, the Dutch East Indies was still in the hands of the Japanese. Japan surrendered on 15 August 1945.

References

Places to Go
Amsterdam: Nederlands Verzetsmuseum
  (Dutch Resistance Museum)
Groesbeek: Nationaal Bevrijdingsmuseum
  (National Liberation Museum)
Hooghalen: Herinneringscentrum Kamp Westerbork
  (Memorial Centre Camp Westerbork)
Overloon: Nationaal Oorlogs- en Verzetsmuseum
  Liberty Park (National War and Resistance
  Museum Liberty Park)
Overveen: Erebegraafplaats Bloemendaal
  (Remembrance Cemetery Bloemendaal)

Websites
www.airbornemuseum.com
www.bevrijdingsmuseum.nl
www.geheugenvannederland.nl
www.kampwesterbork.nl
www.libertypark.nvl
www.minbuza.nl/history/en/1914tot1966,
  1940-1945.html
www.ovmrotterdam.nl
www.verzetsmuseum.org/museum/en/museum

Captions
[page 86] *Seyss-Inquart during his speech to newly-sworn-in army recruits in 1943,* ANP Historisch Archief/F.C. de Haan
[above] *Rotterdam,* May 1940
[beneath] *American and British soldiers, The Battle of Nijmegen,* September 1944, MAI/Sam Presser

1929 - 1945

Anne Frank

The persecution of the Jews

Anne Frank was born into a Jewish family in the German city of Frankfurt am Main in 1929. The family fled to Amsterdam in the summer of 1933. That was the year in which Hitler came to power and began his policy of driving the Jews out of the country.

The Frank family found a house in the Rivierenbuurt in Amsterdam. Anne went to school there and learned Dutch. After the occupation in May 1940, the German authorities implemented measures in the Netherlands aimed at isolating the Jews from the rest of Dutch society. It was a dramatic moment for Anne when she had to say goodbye to her fellow pupils and teacher, because she had been transferred to a Jewish school. Jews were forced to wear a star of David so that they were easily recognisable in public. Signs were hung in cinemas, cafés and theatres stating: "Entry Forbidden to Jews". From July 1942, the German occupation forces implemented a large-scale operation in the Netherlands to transport Jews to Eastern Europe. Jewish families were notified to pack their bags for work in the East. They were collected from their homes, put on trains to the transit camp at Westerbork in the province of Drenthe and from there they were taken to death camps in Eastern Europe. Over 100,000 Jewish men, women and children from the Netherlands died in concentration camps. In total, some six million European Jews were killed in the holocaust.

In 1942, together with four other people, the Frank family went into hiding in a house behind Anne's father's company on the Prinsengracht in Amsterdam. It was here that Anne began to keep the diary which made her famous after the war. She wrote about her experiences as a young, ambitious girl living in a stifling, small room. Later – when she was free again – she wanted to become a writer.

The family managed to stay hidden from the Germans for two years but were then betrayed and captured. Anne died in the German concentration camp Bergen-Belsen in 1945, aged only fifteen. Her sister also died there. Her mother died in Auschwitz. Her father, Otto Frank survived the camp and returned from Poland.

After the war, Miep Gies, a woman who had helped the family when they were in hiding, gave Otto Frank a bundle of exercise books. These were the diaries his daughter Anne had written. Otto Frank took the diaries to several publishers and in 1947 they were published under the title *Het Achterhuis*. (The English title is: Anne Frank: The Diary of a Young Girl.) In 1955, an American stage adaptation of the diaries made the book world famous – just in time to save the actual *Achterhuis* that had been recommended for demolition.

References

Places to Go
Amsterdam: Anne Frankhuis (Anne Frank House)
Amsterdam: Joods Historisch Museum
    (Jewish Historical Museum)
Amsterdam: Verzetsmuseum (Dutch Resistance Museum)
Vught: Nationaal Monument Kamp Vught
    (National Monument Camp Vught)
Westerbork: Herinneringscentrum Kamp Westerbork
    (Memorial Centre Camp Westerbork)

Websites
www.annefrank.ch
www.annefrank.com
www.annefrankguide.net/en-GB
www.annefrank.org.uk
www.annefranktree.com
www.britannica.com/EBchecked/topic/217168
www.jhm.nl
www.kampwesterbork.nl
www.nmkampvught.nl
www.verzetsmuseum.org

Captions
[page 88] *Anne Frank,* AFF Basel/AFS Amsterdam
[top left] *Star of David*
[top right] *"Razzia" (raid) in Amsterdam,* February 1941
[beneath] *The entrance to the Achterhuis*

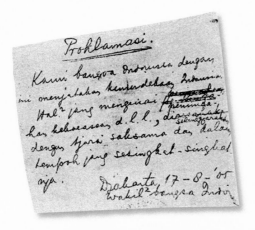

1945 - 1949

Indonesia

A colony fights for freedom

Proklamasi. Kami bangsa Indonesia dengan ini menjatakan kemerdekaan Indonesia...

We, the people of Indonesia, hereby declare the independence of Indonesia...

On 17 August 1945, in a brief ceremony on the streets of Jakarta, Sukarno made a short statement proclaiming to the world that colonial rule of the Dutch East Indies had ended. Two days earlier, Japan had surrendered after the dropping of atomic bombs on the Japanese cities of Hiroshima and Nagasaki. With Japan's surrender, World War II in Asia was brought to an end.

A widespread independence movement had existed in the Dutch East Indies before World War II. Nationalist leaders like Sukarno, Mohammad Hatta and Sutan Sjahrir wanted their country to be free of the Netherlands, others simply wanted more autonomy. The Dutch administration, however, kept a tight hand on the reins.

And then came the Japanese invasion in 1942. On 27 February, the allied forces were defeated in the Java Sea Battle and

their surrender followed on 8 March. The allied troops became prisoners of war, most Dutch citizens were interned in civilian camps, and many men were taken into forced labour. The Japanese dismantled the administration system of the Dutch East Indies and in reality this signalled the end of the existence of the Dutch East Indies.

After 1945, the Netherlands tried to restore its colonial administration through negotiations and with force, in two police actions. However, on 27 December 1949, under a great deal of international pressure, it accepted Indonesian independence. Dutch New Guinea was only relinquished in 1962, and finally, after a transition period under UN supervision and a plebiscite held among the Papuans, the territory was ceded to Indonesia. This meant that from 1969, the national borders of modern-day Indonesia were the same as those of the former Dutch East Indies.

Fighting was heavy during the struggle for independence. By the 1960s, a total of over 300,000 Dutch people, Indo-European, Papuans and Indonesians had left the country. Most of these travelled to the Netherlands. They included 12,500 Moluccan soldiers of the former Royal Netherlands East Indies Army (KNIL) and their families. In 1951, they arrived in the Netherlands where their military service was terminated.

This decolonisation is not yet a thing of the past. In 2005, the Dutch Minister of Foreign Affairs participated in the celebrations surrounding the sixtieth anniversary of Indonesian independence. In this way, the Netherlands accepted that Indonesia had gained independence not in 1949, but on 17 August 1945. Minister Bot expressed regret that the Netherlands at that time "had stood on the wrong side of history, as it were" and had caused a great deal of suffering in so doing. This was an important, sometimes confrontational speech for everyone involved – in Indonesia and the Netherlands alike.

References

Places to Go
Memorials in many Dutch cities, for example in The Hague
Arnhem: Museum Bronbeek
Arnhem: Het Nederlands Openluchtmuseum
   (The Netherlands Open-air Museum)
Amsterdam: Tropenmuseum
Amsterdam: Verzetsmuseum (Dutch Resistance Museum)
Utrecht: Museum Maluku ((history of) Moluccan
   community in the Netherlands)

Websites
www.awm.gov.au/alliesinadversity
www.britannica.com/EBchecked/topic/174553
www.minbuza.nl/history/en/1914tot1966,
   1941---1945.html
www.minbuza.nl/history/en/1914tot1966,
   1945.html
www.museum-maluku.nl
www.openluchtmuseum.nl
www.tropenmuseum.nl
www.verzetsmuseum.org

Captions
[page 90] *Handwritten Proklamasi*, Koninklijk Instituut
   voor de Tropen
[above] *Dutch marines in Indonesia*, 1946,
   Hugo Alexander Wilmar, Rijksmuseum
[beneath] *Sukarno on one of the first Indonesian stamps*

1886 - 1988
Willem Drees
The welfare state

Willem Drees was one of the most popular Prime Ministers in Dutch history. He was known as "Vadertje" (Father Drees) a nickname that shows the socialist Prime Minister was a father figure not only for his own party but for the entire population of the Netherlands. His enormous popularity was largely due to the emergency law on state old-age pensions he implemented in 1947.

At an early age, Drees joined the Social Democratic Workers' party (SDAP), the predecessor of the Dutch Labour Party (PvdA). He experienced the crisis years of the 1930s as an alderman in The Hague and tried to alleviate the effects for municipal employees. After the war, Drees entered the cabinet as Minister of Social Affairs. From 1948 to 1958 he was Prime Minister of the Christian Democrat and Social Democrat coalition (*rooms-rode coalitie*).

Stories about Willem Drees always mention his thriftiness and simplicity. The most important politician in the Netherlands went to work every morning either on foot or by bicycle – he did not need a chauffeur-driven car. At the time, most politicians enjoyed cigars and drinking, but Drees refrained. And when an American diplomat visited Drees at home to discuss American financial support for the Dutch economy, Mrs Drees apparently served him a cup of tea and a biscuit. The American supposedly said that a country with such a thrifty Prime Minister was undoubtedly greatly in need of assistance through the Marshall Plan.

Drees was closely tied to the years in which the Netherlands was recovering from World War II. The economy had to be kick-started and everyone had to lend a hand. The emphasis was placed on cooperation rather than conflict. Employees agreed to low wages to achieve a competitive position for the Netherlands in respect of other countries. This meant that most people had to postpone buying a car or a television set. In politics, cooperation was the top priority, even though pillarisation was ingrained in Dutch society during those years and most of the Dutch lived their lives within their own small social circle. Catholic boys joined a Catholic football club, socialists joined a socialist hiking association.

The Drees cabinets were broad-based, with Catholics and socialists having the most sway. Together, they built the Dutch welfare state. The best-known measure from that time is the state Old-age Pension Act (AOW) of 1956, which Drees initiated in 1947 with his emergency law for the elderly. Every elderly person over the age of 65 received a pension from the state. Pensioners at the time talked about "drawing money from Drees" as if he were paying them out of his own pocket. When Willem Drees died in 1988, he was 101 years old, so he certainly had time to enjoy his old-age pension.

93

References

Places to Go
Amsterdam: Rijsmuseum
(when the museum is fully accessable again (its renovation is estimated to be complete in 2012), the office of Drees will be on display)
Arnhem: Openluchtmuseum (Open-air Museum)
The Hague: Binnenhof (seat of the Dutch Parliament in Drees' time)

Websites
www.britannica.com/EBchecked/topic/171299/Willem-Drees
www.openluchtmuseum.nl
www.rijksmuseum.nl

Captions
[page 92] *Willem Drees Sr.,* Internationaal Instituut voor Sociale Geschiedenis/BG B27/653
[right] In 1954, the status of the Netherlands West Indies was upgraded from a colonial territory to a part of the Kingdom of the Netherlands as a separate country within the kingdom. Spaarnestad Photo/Hollandse Hoogte

1 February 1953
The great flood
The danger of water

Late in the night of 31 January 1953, the dykes of the province of Zeeland gave way during an enormous storm: 1,835 people lost their lives, 72,000 people lost their homes and 200,000 hectares of land were flooded. A national disaster. Across the whole of the Netherlands, money and clothing was collected, evacuees were warmly welcomed and aid arrived from abroad.

The disaster could have been much worse. If the dykes of the province of South Holland had not held, another 30,000 might have drowned and a further one million would have been made homeless. Because, behind these dykes, close to the Dutch IJssel, lies the lowest part of the Netherlands. The waters would have reached levels of over seven metres in most places if these dykes had burst.

To prevent such a disaster reoccurring, soon after the flood, work was begun on the Delta works storm surge barrier.

Plans had been made earlier to strengthen coastal flood barriers, but due to the war and post-war reconstruction they had not been implemented yet. All the gaps between the islands were closed by dams. The sea and river dykes were strengthened and a storm surge barrier was built in the Dutch IJssel.

As they went along, the engineers realised that not all the arms of the river should be sealed off because this would cause the unique natural environment to disappear. For this reason, a storm surge barrier was built in the Oosterschelde with openings that are only closed in the event of an emergency. The Wester-schelde could not be sealed off from the sea, because it provides access to the ports of Antwerp and Ghent. Consequently, the sea dykes were simply reinforced here.

Thanks to this enormous project, the south-western Netherlands is much more secure against flooding than ever before. At the same time, new bridges and dams have improved the accessibility of the islands of Zeeland, which has fostered the development of industry and tourism in the province.

The great flood of 1953 clearly illustrated how vulnerable large areas of the Netherlands were to flooding. It is now known that the danger is not only from the sea, but from the great rivers as well. Climate change is causing rainfall in Europe to become unpredictable and this affects the water levels of the great rivers. In 1993 and 1995, the situation in the Netherlands was critical: some of the great rivers were on the point of flooding. This led to the implementation of a large number of projects to strengthen the dykes. However, experts believe that just raising the dykes is not the solution. They think that the rivers should be given more room, that building on river-forelands should be stopped and that areas should be designated for the temporary storage of excess water. This philosophy translates into learning to live with water and not in conflict with it.

References

Places to Go
A drive over the 1.8 mile long Oosterscheldekering
    (storm surge barrier Oosterschelde).
Ouwerkerk: Watersnoodmuseum
    (Flood disaster Museum)
Vrouwenpolder: Deltapark Neeltje Jans

Websites
www.deltawerken.com
www.minbuza.nl/history/en/1914tot1966,1953.html
www.neeltjejans.nl/index.php/en/home
www.watersnoodmuseum.nl
www.zijpermuseum.nl

Captions
[page 94] *Small boat,* unknown
[left] *Dreischen,* unknown
[top right] *Rescue by a soldier,* unknown
[beneath right] *Rescue by a soldier,* unknown

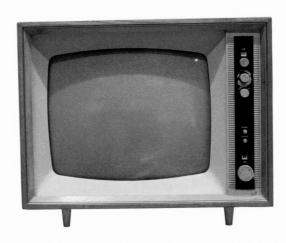

1948 - the present

Television

The rise of mass media

In the 1950s, the Philips company was one of the driving forces behind the introduction of television in the Netherlands. In advertising campaigns, the Eindhoven-based company praised the new medium as a phenomenon that did not pose a threat to the traditional family but would rather strengthen it. The advertisements often showed a happy and harmonious family watching the screen that was bringing the world into their living room.

In order to capture a segment of the European market, Philips first had to sell a sufficient number of sets in its own country. To this end, in 1948 the company began the experiment of broadcasting programs that could be received in Eindhoven and the surrounding area. In 1951, radio broadcasting corporations in Bussum took up the television experiment. The densely-populated western Netherlands was now receiving broadcasts with the full support of Philips.

In those days of thriftiness and diligence, Prime Minister Drees attempted to limit private spending, but by the end of the fifties this innovation could no longer be resisted. By about 1961, one million television sets were in use in the Netherlands and around twenty hours a week of programs were being broadcast. The news, dramas, entertainment and sporting events were popular viewing. Around 1970, virtually every household in the country had a black and white set and some had even moved on to colour.

The arrival of the television caused great changes in the living room. The focus was no longer on the dining table because everyone had to have a good view of the TV from the sofa or an easy chair, preferably with a side table nearby with snacks and a drink. The use of leisure time was also affected. By around 1970, the average Dutch person watched about one and a half hours of television a day and spent much less time on activities like playing cards and board games. Critics believed that this viewing behaviour would lead to passivity and encourage slavish consumerism. Supporters of the new medium, however, pointed out the fun that families had while watching together and the informative function served by television. Television also played an important role in shaping opinions on social topics. Due to the limited viewing choice (until 1964 there was only one channel, and only two thereafter), many people used to watch the same programmes. When they arrived at work the next morning, they had something to discuss. Programs about controversial issues like sex, emancipation, youth culture, religion and the royal family invited a lot of discussion.

With the introduction of cable and satellite television, the range of programs on offer became much broader and more international. Today, most people spend more hours watching television than people in 1970 did, but watching television as a family activity is less common, due in part to the fact that a great many children have their own television sets. This individualisation has continued with the advent of the internet, that offers an even wider window through which to view the world.

PHILIPS **TELEVISIE**
verrijkt het gezinsleven!

References

Places to Go
Hilversum: Nederlands Instituut voor Beeld en Geluid
    (Dutch Institute of Picture and Sound)

Websites
www.educatie.beeldengeluid.nl
www.philips.com/about/company/history/index.page

Captions
[page 96] *Television,* Bradley Mason
[left] *Philips brochure,* Philips Company Archives
[right] *A Dutch family watching TV,* 1950

The port of Rotterdam

Gateway to the world

If there is one place that has made the Netherlands such an important trading nation in modern times, it is Rotterdam. The port lies at the delta of major European rivers, is accessible for sea-going ships and currently has access to a market of one hundred million people just a day's drive away. It is the natural location for Europe's major port. The rebuilding of the port was therefore a top priority during the post-war reconstruction of the Netherlands. The port was severely damaged in World War II – almost half of it was destroyed. Due in part to the re-emergence of Germany and successful European cooperation, trade with the German market was restored. Growth was so swift that by the 1950s expansion of the port was needed: the Eemshaven and Botlek were developed.

Rotterdam had only become the major port of the Netherlands in the nineteenth century. Although the city had existed for a long time, it had not been considered a top priority port. In around 1250, a dam was built in the estuary of the small Rotte River to prevent inflowing seawater from making the river-water too salty. At the dam, goods were loaded by hand from riverboats onto coasters – this was the beginning of the port of Rotterdam. In the sixteenth century, Rotterdam developed into an important fishing port and later the city had some share of the colonial expeditions. However, Rotterdam never became the centre of colonial trade: the port at that time was too difficult to reach from the sea and moreover, the major financiers and entrepreneurs had their offices in Amsterdam.

In the second half of the nineteenth century, the port changed dramatically. Mining and industry began to flourish in the German *Ruhrgebiet*. Furthermore, Rotterdam became much more easy to reach from the sea. Under the direction of hydraulic engineer Pieter Caland, the dunes at the Hook of Holland were cut through and a new link was dug to the port: the *Nieuwe Waterweg* (New Waterway). In the port itself, new harbour basins were dug. Steam cranes and other machinery facilitated loading and unloading, and freight trains transported the products quickly.

The port of Rotterdam has grown continuously over the past forty years, for example, with the development of the *Europoort* and the *Maasvlakte*. It is important to the Netherlands government to keep the port of Rotterdam competitive.

Just like Schiphol Airport, Rotterdam is a main port, a hub for Dutch international trade relations. Today, globalisation means that goods are transported intensively from one end of the globe to the other. Competition is increasing – even between ports. For this reason the state is paying extra attention to the design and accessibility of the port of Rotterdam. The *Betuwelijn*, a new freight railway line between Rotterdam and Germany, is one of the projects that will lay the foundations for the future of the port.

References

Places to Go
Rotterdam: a boattrip in the harbour
Rotterdam: Havenmuseum (Harbourmuseum)
Rotterdam: Maritiem Museum Rotterdam
    (Maritime Museum Rotterdam)
Rotterdam: visit the Wereldhavendagen
    (Worldharbourdays), yearly in August or September

Websites
www.havenmuseum.nl
www.maritiemmuseum.nl
www.portofrotterdam.com/en/home/

Captions
[page 98] *OOCL container ship in the port of Rotterdam*, ANP/Robin Utrecht
[above] *Unloading a container ship*, Teun van den Dries
[right] *The Erasmus bridge against the skyline of Rotterdam*, Willem Schulte

Annie M.G. Schmidt
Pluk van de Petteflet
Met illustraties van Fiep Westendorp
Querido

1911 - 1995

Annie M.G. Schmidt

Going against the grain of a bourgeois country

"Never do what your mother tells you to do, then everything will be alright." These words are typical of the Dutch writer Annie M.G. Schmidt. They are a fine example of why so many of her verses, songs, books, plays, musicals and radio plays are both sparkling fresh and comically rebellious.

Annie was born in Zuid-Beveland in 1911. The daughter of a clergyman, she was a precocious child, and she examined the world around her with a somewhat surprised look in her eyes. She wrote her first verses of poetry when she was fourteen. After World War II, she went to work for the Amsterdam newspaper *Het Parool*, where she met the illustrator Fiep Westendorp. From 1952 to 1957 they worked together on a series of children's

stories about a boy and a girl, Jip and Janneke [Jim and Jennifer], that were published each day in the newspaper. This marked the beginning of a lifelong collaboration that resulted in books such as *Pluk van de Petteflet*, *Otje* and *Floddertje*.

In the 1950s, Annie had enormous success with her fortnightly radio series *De familie Doorsnee* [The Average Family]. Everyone in the Netherlands listened to the series, regardless of which socio-political group they belonged to. The ups and downs of this family portrayed the contemporary life of Dutch families after the war. Annie also captured the spirit of the times in other works like her lyrics for cabaret shows and later in musicals. Her first television series "*Pension Hommeles*" [Bicker's Boarding House] was screened and was followed by the legendary series "*Ja zuster, nee zuster*" [Yes, sister, No, sister], that was adapted for the big screen in 2002. Annie M.G. Schmidt's rebellious texts made her one of the most influential, and at the same time most gentle critics of the respectable, bourgeois and pillarised Netherlands.

Through her work, Annie M.G. Schmidt inspired many children and adults. Millions of copies of *Jip en Janneke* alone have been sold and her writing has been translated into numerous languages. Her publisher referred to her as "the true Queen of the Netherlands". When he asked her to hold a book-signing session at the *Uitmarkt* in Amsterdam, the organisers asked him to never do it again: the narrow lanes and alleys of Amsterdam could not cope with the crowds and congestion. The secret of her success? "I have always been eight years old. And I actually write for myself. I think that is the point. I am eight."

References

Places to Go
The Hague: Letterkundig Museum
(Literature Museum)

Websites
www.annie-mg.com/huiskamer/about_annie/index.html

Captions
[page 100] *Cover of Pluk van de Petteflet,*
Fiep Westendorp, Em. Querido's Uitgeverij BV
[top left] *Jip and Janneke*, Fiep Westendorp, Illustre BV
[beneath left] *A statue of Jip and Janneke in Zaltbommel*
[top right] *Annie M.G. Schmidt*, Steye Raviez/
Hollandse Hoogte
[beneath right] *A Chinese edition of Jip and Janneke*

1945 - the present
Surinam and the Netherlands Antilles
Decolonisation in the West

The colourful architecture of Willemstad, the capital of Curaçao, bears witness to the history of this port and trade centre since 1635. Curaçao is one of the six Antillian islands that form part of the Kingdom of the Netherlands, together with Aruba, Bonaire, Saba, St. Martin and St. Eustatius. Up until 1975, Surinam was also included.

The relationships between the Netherlands and its colonies in the "West" changed drastically in the second half of the twentieth century. During World War II, Surinam and the Netherlands Antilles remained free. They provided military support to allied operations and supplied raw materials needed for the war industry, like bauxite and petroleum. After the war, the so-called overseas territories were granted regional autonomy and the right to vote. This new relationship was set down in the Charter for the Kingdom of the Netherlands (*Statuut voor het Koninkrijk der Nederlanden*) enacted in 1954, a type of constitution for a transatlantic kingdom with autonomous overseas territories.

In the early 1970s, many African and Asian countries had already been decolonised and in Surinam too the movement for independence began to gather momentum. The Netherlands, under the leadership of Labour Prime Minister Joop den Uyl, immediately supported this movement. Within two years, together with Henck Arron (Prime Minister of the ruling coalition party in Surinam), Den Uyl had drawn up an arrangement for arriving at independence. After weathering heavy opposition led by Jagernath Lachmon, finally, on 25 November 1975, the arrangement resulted in the unanimous acceptance of independence. The Netherlands agreed to continue to support Surinam with development funding for a long period. These payments were suspended for a few years following the 1982 "December Murders".

In 1975, the tensions between the different ethnic groups in the run-up to independence, uncertainty about the future and the choice each inhabitant had to make between either Surinamese or Dutch nationality, led to the departure from Surinam of over 130,000 Surinamese for the Netherlands. The Charter of 1954 continued to govern the relationship between the Netherlands and the Antilles. Within this framework, in 1986 Aruba was granted *Status Aparte* (separate status) and since 1996 it has been a nation within the Kingdom. Since 2005, discussions have been held with the other islands about revising their relationships.

In many ways, through their long common history, family ties and the Dutch language, the Netherlands has strong trans-national links with the multicultural Caribbean societies of Surinam, the Netherlands Antilles and Aruba. Many languages are spoken in those regions, but they all have the Dutch language in common. In 2005 Surinam became a member of the *Nederlandse Taalunie* [Dutch Language Union], alongside the Netherlands and Belgium/Flanders.

References

Places to Go

Amsterdam: Imagine IC
(Image, identity and culture centre)
Amsterdam: Kwakoefestival (multicultural festival, held every Saturday and Sunday in July and August)
Amsterdam: Tropenmuseum
Delft: Nusantara Museum (museum about history and cultures of Indonesia)
Rotterdam: Zomercarnaval
(multicultural summer carnival, held in July)
The Hague: Sarnamihuis (Sarnami House, history and culture of Hindus in the Netherlands and Suriname)

Websites

www.britannica.com/EBchecked/topic/575240
www.imagineic.nl/english
www.minbuza.nl/history/en/1967tot2000,1975.html
www.zomercarnaval.nl/nl/English

Captions

[page 102] *Willemstad waterfront, Curacao,*
Brand X Pictures/Hollandse Hoogte
[left] *Prime Minister Den Uyl and Prime Minister Arron*
sign the declaration of independence, 1975
[right] *Raising of the flag ceremony in the Suriname*
Stadium leads to exuberant celebrations among VIPs,
Center Queen Beatrix, ANP Historisch Archief

Srebrenica

The dilemmas of peacekeeping

On 9 July 1995, the Bosnian Serb troops of General Mladic moved towards the Dutchbat III protected enclave of Srebrenica. Without too much resistance the attacking troops took control of this safe-haven for Muslims. The Serbs had the Muslims removed in buses, after first separating the men from the women and children with assistance from the Dutch forces. A short time later, the Serbs executed most of the men (at least 7000). The Dutch soldiers, some of whom suspected what was to come but none of whom witnessed the executions, were given safe passage to Zagreb, where they were welcomed by Prime Minister Kok and Crown Prince Willem-Alexander.

When news of the massacre that had taken place "under the very eyes of Dutchbat" reached the Netherlands, the question was raised as to whether the Dutch soldiers should have protected the enclave against the Bosnian Serb troops ands so avoided the slaughter. Initially, attention was largely focused on the troops, but it soon became clear that responsibility could not be laid at their feet. Their mandate prohibited them from participating in the war. In September 1996, the Netherlands Institute for War Documentation (NIOD) was commissioned by the government to investigate the exact circumstances of the incident. When the NIOD report was published in 2002, Prime Minister Kok accepted political responsibility for the massacre in Srebrenica and resigned.

Right from the outset, Dutch soldiers have participated in UN peacekeeping missions whereby, on behalf of the United Nations, troops supervise compliance with peace treaties and ceasefires in various troubled areas around the globe. The first mission was in 1948, in Israel. A recurring problem during these missions is the instruction on the use of force.

What are the peacekeepers allowed to do, and what is prohibited in these trouble spots? The Dutch Lower House has the ultimate say in instructing Dutch troops. The House has to endorse the agreements made between the government and the UN regarding the degree to which the troops are armed and the type of force they are permitted to use. This means that the balance between the duties of Dutch troops and the dangers they consequently run is ultimately struck in the Dutch Lower House. After the massacre at Srebrenica, it was once again set down that the House must be kept as well informed as possible in this regard.

The aftershocks of Srebrenica were felt deeply in the Netherlands. It led to increased hesitation and more caution when deploying Dutch troops abroad. However, the incident did not result in the Netherlands sitting on the fence and rejecting international requests for military support, because the Netherlands desires to continue to play a role in international politics and peacekeeping.

105

N.B. The canon committee hesitated before including this window. Not so much because the underlying story is so complex, or unflattering, to put it mildly, to the Netherlands. We have faith in the capacity of primary school teachers to explain this to their pupils, and a canon has to pay its dues to the blacker moments of history too. It is, however, the case that thanks to the internet, the most horrific images of the drama in Srebrenica are only a mouse-click away. Although the truth is undoubtedly served by this, the committee would like to warn teachers and other staff about the attendant risks.

References

Places to Go
Delft: Legermuseum (Army Museum)
The Hague: Nederlandse Veteranendag (Dutch Veterans Day, every year on the last Saturday of June)

Websites
www.britannica.com/EBchecked/topic/561873
www.un.org/peace

Captions
[page 104] *Dutchbat in Srebrenica,* Ministry of Defence
[left] *Dutchbat in Srebrenica,* Nederlands Instituut voor Militaire Historie
[right] *Burial of 308 identified Bosnians, July 2008,* Conor Smith Gaffney

1945 - the present

Diversity in the Netherlands
The multicultural society

On 1 January 2000, the twentieth century passed into history and the twenty-first century began. While over five million people lived in the Netherlands in 1900, on New Year's Day 2000 this number had grown to 15,864,000 according to figures from Statistics Netherlands. Some 1,598,200 of these were children attending primary school.

In the Netherlands, there are many types of primary schools, due among other things, to differences in religion and ideology. In addition to public schools, there are, for example, Protestant, Roman Catholic, Jewish, Islamic, Hindu, Humanist and Anthroposophist schools. In principle, the curriculum is equivalent at all of these schools. However, the lessons concerned with religion and ideology are different. Because religion can also have an effect on clothing and behaviour, on rituals and religious holidays, schools can also differ from one another in these respects. Parents choose the schools for their children for their own reasons.

Pupils themselves know exactly which school they attend.

Diversity in education, on the grounds of ideology or teaching methods, has existed throughout the twentieth century. Freedom of education is set down in Article 23 of the Dutch Constitution. The decision to regard privately-run schools as equal to public schools was opposed in what came to be known as the school funding controversy. This controversy had long been settled and, as a result of the secularisation, was all but forgotten, when, in 1988 and 1989, the first Hindu and Islamic primary schools were set up.

This founding of new schools arose from changes in the composition of the Dutch population. After 1945, the Netherlands had been an emigration country with its people leaving for Australia, Canada, the United States and South Africa, while its immigrants came largely from the former Dutch East Indies. From the beginning of the 1960s, an active immigration policy resulted in the arrival of immigrant workers from countries like Italy, Spain, the former Yugoslavia, Turkey and Morocco, to fill jobs in Dutch industry. They brought their families with them. The Netherlands, like many other European countries, also offered asylum to political refugees and opened its borders within Europe.

In this way, the diversity of Dutch society increased rapidly in a short space of time. As recently as 1955, for example, the first mosque in the Netherlands was established in The Hague. By 2000, Islam in the Netherlands, just like Christianity, had many different branches and the minaret is now a well-known city image. Since the beginning of the twenty-first century, a new kind of school funding controversy has been raging, largely around new Islamic schools. This reflects the fierce political debate about the relationship between society, culture and religion that is being conducted on numerous themes: from major political issues to the problems of everyday life. Time and again the question of what "being Dutch" actually entails is raised. The current, diverse generation of young Dutch residents who are attending school now will be the ones to add substance to the answer.

References

Places to Go
Visit a church, a synagogue, a mosque or any other religious site
Have dinner in a restaurant that serves non-European food
Visit a market in a big city, and taste the non-European food that is for sale at the stalls
Rotterdam: Dunya Festival (non-European music), yearly in May

Websites
www.britannica.com/EBchecked/topic/941150
www.forum.nl/english/index.html

Captions
[page 106] *Community centre children's afternoon,* Chris Pennarts/Hollandse Hoogte
[left] *Mevlana mosque in Rotterdam,* Nick Hannes/Hollandse Hoogte
[right] *The Dutch National Soccerteam,* 2007

The natural gas deposit
A finite treasure

It has been called the raft on which the Dutch economy and prosperity floats: the enormous gas field that was discovered in 1959 near Slochteren in the province of Groningen. It is estimated that more than 300 billion cubic metres of gas lie in the ground here: the second-largest deposit of gas known at the time. It is now known that the field contains 3000 billion cubic metres of gas. Thanks to this discovery, the Netherlands has gradually switched over to gas completely. Almost every household uses natural gas, and over ten thousand glasshouses and some five thousand businesses are connected to the natural gas network.

The so-called "gas pocket" is not actually a pocket. The gas is trapped in porous rock underground. It is sealed from above by a layer of impermeable rock (otherwise the gas would have escaped into the atmosphere long ago). As the gas is extracted, the rock simply stays where it is. And yet, during large-scale gas extraction, slight earth tremors may occur caused by underground subsidence, which can lead to cracks in walls or roads.

For the Dutch government, natural gas is a source of revenue. The state has a profit share. The price of natural gas is linked to the price of oil, and as the oil price continues to rise, so to do the revenues from natural gas. The question is: how long can the Netherlands continue to profit from this natural source of energy? According to the Nederlandse Aardolie Maatschappij (Netherlands Petroleum Company; NAM), that deals with extracting the gas, the reserves are sufficient for at least a further twenty-five years of high-level production. However, the NAM believes that it will gradually become more difficult to meet all obligations. Dutch and foreign customers would have to be served, in peak-demand periods as well, while the pressure in the Slochteren field is already reducing significantly. The technical problems involved in continuing to extract large volumes of gas from the field will become increasingly greater.

It is for good reason that the NAM would like to begin operations in new fields, including under the Wadden Sea, something to which some environmental organisations are violently opposed. Their objections are not aimed at the use of natural gas – it is a clean fuel – but rather at the disturbance of the tranquillity of the Wadden Sea, the most important nature reserve in the Netherlands – and at skyline pollution, and, in particular, subsidence in the area. The major lobbyist for the area, the Wadden Society, has agreed to operations being implemented with the proviso that this takes place under stringent conditions.

Future generations will be faced with difficult political choices.

Can the Netherlands manage without revenues from natural gas? Can the country, if the worst comes to the worst, convert to alternative energy sources? Should the Netherlands import more foreign natural gas and store it in its gas fields? And as far as the Wadden Sea is concerned: does nature conservation deserve a higher priority than economic gain, are gas revenues more important than the environment or can the quality of the environment and gas extraction be combined in an acceptable manner?

References

Places to Go
Petten: Energieonderzoek Centrum Nederland
(Dutch energy research centre)

Websites
www.cedelft.nl/eng
www.ecn.nl/en
www.minbuza.nl/history/en/1914tot1966,1959.html
www.nam.nl
www.senternovem.nl/english
www.waddenvereniging.nl

Captions
[page 108] *Burner on a gas hob,* Rob Huibers/
Hollandse Hoogte
[left] *Flare and drum,* N.A.M.
[right] *Pipelines,* N.A.M.
[beneath] *The Wadden Sea at low tide,*
Merijn van der Vliet

1945 - the present

Europe

The Dutch and Europeans

The Netherlands does not exist in isolation. It is closely tied to its neighbouring countries and together they form Europe. After World War II, the heads of state of a number of western European countries realised that the future of Europe lay in cooperation, to prevent another war breaking out. It started with cooperation in the area of strategic resources. Around 1950, these resources were coal and steel. At the time, coal was the major energy source, and steel was needed in large amounts to reconstruct the infrastructure of western Europe. Six European countries signed the Treaty of Paris in 1951, and by doing so established the European Coal and Steel Community (ECSC). This treaty allowed for, among other things, free trade in these resources between the six participating nations: the Netherlands, Belgium, Luxembourg, France, Germany and Italy.

In 1957, the six nations took the next step by signing the Treaty of Rome. This made the European Economic Community (EEC) a reality: a customs union of the six member countries that guaranteed free trade in all products. The EEC quickly launched a common agricultural policy aimed at safeguarding the provision of food and improving the incomes of farmers. The Treaty also established the European Atomic Energy Community (better known as Euratom), a third European community, focused on the exploration and development of nuclear energy for peaceful purposes. Later, the three Communities were merged into a single European Community; today, it is referred to as the European Union (EU).

This European cooperation was a success in many ways. Numerous other European nations wished to join. The first new members were the United Kingdom, Denmark and Ireland (1973), followed later by southern European enlargement with the addition of Greece (1981) and Spain and Portugal (1986). In 1995, Austria, Finland and Sweden joined, bringing the number of member states to fifteen. The biggest enlargement took place in 2004 when eight countries from the former Eastern Bloc acceded to the European Union along with Malta and Cyprus. In 2007, the EU member states number twenty-five and further enlargement is around the corner.

A European Union comprising ever more countries is also an EU of more and more votes, interests and cultures. This makes it increasingly difficult to agree on the future aims of the EU and on the priorities for European cooperation as shown by the Dutch rejection of the proposals for a European Constitution. For the Netherlands, a future without Europe is virtually unimaginable. The vast majority of the nation's trade takes place within Europe. The various economies of the EU are strongly interwoven and the freedom of movement of workers regularly reminds the Dutch (and others) that we are all part of Europe and we are all Europeans.

References

Places to Go
Brussels (Belgium): a visit to the European Parliament
Brussels (Belgium): Musée de l'Europe
(Museum of Europe)

Websites
www.britannica.com/EBchecked/topic/196399
http://europa.eu/index_en.htm
www.eustudies.org
www.lib.berkeley.edu/doemoff/govinfo/intl/gov_eu.html
www.minbuza.nl/history/en/2001to2005,2005.html
www.minbuza.nl/history/en/2001to2005,2002.html
(the Euro)
www.mun.ca/ceuep/EU-bib.html

Captions
[page 110] *Euro coin,* Koninklijke Nederlandse Munt
[above] *The European Parliament in Brussels*

Main lines of the canon

Introductory explanation: characteristics of the main lines

- It is important that certain terms like "the Netherlands", "Dutch culture" and "Dutch history" are used with caution. After all, up until the nineteenth century the term "the Netherlands" is an anachronism and the adjective "Dutch" remains problematic in early history. When a text mentions the history of Dutch language and culture, and Dutch territory and the Dutch state, we actually mean "relevant to this region", without the suggestion that this region in that time already presented a cultural, political or linguistic unity. We have treated these matters as historical phenomena.

- In the texts, Dutch history and culture are not treated as isolated components but rather they are described within the context of developments in Europe and the rest of the world.

- The structure of the main lines is roughly chronological, although it should be pointed out that certain aspects (for example, the struggle against the water or Christian culture) cannot be restricted to one single period.

- The main lines provide orientation in time and place: they sketch a general picture of what the previous generations that inhabited this region would have experienced.

Main lines of the canon of Dutch history and culture

Introduction

These fourteen "main lines of the canon" are meant to serve as background texts to the fifty windows. They are the red threads running through the history of the Netherlands that indicate the cross-links between the separate windows, thereby helping to create cohesion in the topics, objects, persons and themes featured on the chart.

1 The Low Countries by the sea

The modern-day Netherlands was largely "created" by human hands: dyked-in, reclaimed and developed. Adapting to and struggling against water is a red thread in the history of this region.

→ **The Beemster polder • The great flood**

2 On the periphery of Europe

The region that is today known as the Netherlands is a river delta on the periphery of the European continent. This geographic position has determined the history of the region throughout the centuries. In 4500 BC, an agrarian society began to develop here, and from the beginning of the Christian era the region formed one of the frontiers of the Roman Empire. In later centuries, the region became part of other large empires. It was only from about 1590 that the first contours of the modern-day Netherlands began to be mapped. However, the borders would often be changed dramatically.

→ **The Roman Limes • Charlemagne • Charles V**

3 A converted country

Little is known about the religion of the earliest inhabitants of the region, but thanks to Tacitus (among others) we do know something about the gods that the people here honoured. The people of the low countries converted to Christianity from about 600-700 AD. Monasteries became centres of culture. In the sixteenth and seventeenth centuries, wars were waged in the name of the true doctrine. Today, Christianity still remains an important feature of Dutch culture.

→ **Megalithic tombs • The Roman Limes • Willibrord • Erasmus • The *Beeldenstorm* • The *Statenbijbel***

4 A Dutch language

The earliest extant words written in Dutch date from circa 1100. They were written by a Flemish monk. Printed material in the "mother tongue" only became available in the sixteenth century. Many people continued to speak and write in Latin (scientists) and in French (the elite). Regions had their own dialects. And yet the Netherlands has a long history of literature in its own language. The borders of language do not run parallel to political borders.

→ **Hebban olla vogala** • **The *Statenbijbel*** • *Max Havelaar* •
Annie M.G. Schmidt

5 An urbanised country and a trading hub at the mouth of the Rhine, Schelde and Maas rivers

From circa 1100, urbanisation began to take place in the region and trading centres were established. The centre of gravity initially lay in the south (Flanders and Brabant), but by circa 1500 the north (province of Holland) was a strong centre of trade. From circa 1600, the provinces of Holland and Zeeland were important hubs for trade in Europe. The modern-day Netherlands continues to fulfil this function.

→ **The Hanseatic League** • **The canal ring** • **The port of Rotterdam**

6 The Republic of the Seven United Netherlands: founded on rebellion

Towns, with their citizens, have different interests than the nobility. The first signs of a clash of these interests could be seen early. In the late Middle Ages, the Burgundian rulers tried to bring the Low Countries under one administration, but this policy met with resistance from both town-dwellers and the nobility. In the sixteenth century, this resistance blended with the call for Reformation. War broke out and the nobility became "gueux'. William of Orange rose to become the leader of the Rebellion and for this reason is known as the "father of the fatherland". The unique political structure known as the "Republic" developed after his violent death in 1584. Features of the Republic: the administrative power of regents; weak central authority; religious tolerance.

→ **Floris V** • **Charles V** • **The *Beeldenstorm*** • **William of Orange** •
The Republic • **Hugo Grotius** • **Spinoza** • **The canal ring**

7 The blossoming of the Golden Age

The Republic of the Seven United Netherlands was a superpower in Europe in the seventeenth century: economically, politically and culturally. The period was short but intense. Immigrants (Jews, Flemings, Huguenots) played an important role in this blossoming.

In the cultural domain, the scope and quality of seventeenth-century painting was particularly remarkable. Economically, it was shipping, the staple market, the highly-developed land cultivation and industry. Politically, the Republic had a unique form of government on a continent where monarchies were the rule. The disaster year of 1672 signalled the beginning of the end for this period of previously unknown blossoming. Thereafter, the Republic was a humble player on the European stage, dependent on the European powers for room to manoeuvre. In economic and cultural terms, the Republic was also less of a European player from the end of the seventeenth century.

→ **Hugo Grotius • Rembrandt • Michiel de Ruyter • Blaeu's** *Atlas Major* **• Christiaan Huygens • Spinoza • Country mansions**

8 Business sense and colonial power

Dutch ships took to the seas from about 1600. Europe was the world's centre of trade, but business was conducted in Asia, Africa and America as well. Colonies were established in Asia and America. The Dutch also traded in slaves on all three continents. In the nineteenth century, the centralisation of the Dutch administration of the colonies led to lengthy wars. To this day, the Netherlands still maintains strong ties with Indonesia, Surinam and the Antilles.

→ **The VOC • Blaeu's** *Atlas Major* **• Slavery •** *Max Havelaar* **• Indonesia • Surinam and the Antilles • Diversity in the Netherlands**

9 Nation-state, constitutional monarchy

In the second half of the eighteenth century, due to the influence of the Enlightenment, among other things, the need arose among a broad range of people to acquire and disseminate knowledge. New ideas about the organisation of the state and society were discussed. The patriot movement's attempts to limit the power of the Stadholders (governors) and to give the people a greater voice were initially unsuccessful.

The modern-day Dutch state was formed between 1795 and 1848. The foundations of the nation-state were laid in the French period (1795-1813). After the defeat of Napoleon, William I, the son of the last Stadholder (governor) became king of a united kingdom. This "restoration" of the Netherlands did not last long, because Brussels joined in the rebellions of the year 1830. In 1848, the foundations for a constitutional monarchy (as the Netherlands still is today) were laid with the drafting of the Constitution by Thorbecke. The kingdom became minor power that cherishes its neutrality.

→ **Country mansions • Eise Eisinga • The patriots • Napoleon Bonaparte • King William I • The Constitution**

10 The rise of modern society

From circa 1870, Amsterdam, Rotterdam, The Hague and Utrecht began to grow into cities. Industrialisation reached the region relatively late. The laying of the first railways began somewhat earlier. Distances became smaller: the integration of the Netherlands had begun.

The call for equality under the law became stronger. "Common" citizens demanded their say in society and politics. This resulted in universal suffrage being granted to men and women in 1917 and 1919 respectively. "Modern" artists of the time no longer regarded themselves as the keepers of established artistic traditions and reveal themselves as artistic innovators. In literature this goal is reflected in the "Movement of the Eighties", in painting, in Impressionism and Post-impressionism and in the applied art of the Art Nouveau and Modernism movements.

→ **The first railway • Opposition to child labour • Vincent van Gogh • Aletta Jacobs • World War I • *De Stijl***

11 The Netherlands in a time of World War 1914-1945

As a small country, the Netherlands tried to avoid involvement in large conflicts in Europe. It succeeded during World War I, but at its end, the Netherlands was dragged into a world crisis. The blackest moments of the German occupation were the bombing of Rotterdam, the deportation and murder of the Jewish population and the winter of starvation. In Asia, the war began in 1942, but after the liberation of 1945 a new war began that lasted until 1949. World War II is referred to as "the past that refuses to become history".

→ **World War I • *De Stijl* • The crisis years • World War II • Anne Frank • Indonesia**

12 The welfare state, democratisation and secularisation

Reconstruction began immediately after the end of World War II. After those years of deprivation and hard work, the 1950s heralded in a period of great change in the lifestyle of the Dutch population. The welfare state and an affluent society ensured a radical rise in the standard of living. In addition, people were breaking their ties with their church, socio-political group and family. This change was marked in particular by less hierarchical relationships between parents and children, the rise of new male and female role patterns and increasingly open views on sexuality. In terms of politics, this was combined with a strong movement towards democratisation: the authority of established, elite groups was called into question.

→ **Willem Drees • The great flood • Television • The port of Rotterdam • Annie M.G. Schmidt • The natural gas deposit**

13 The diversification of the Netherlands

After World War II, the Netherlands became embroiled in a colonial war with the Indonesian independence movement. During and after this war, many Dutch, Indo-Europeans, and Moluccans left for the Netherlands. Other immigration waves followed: in the 1960s, workers from Mediterranean countries arrived, at the time of the decolonisation of Surinam (1975) people arrived from the former colony and later from the Netherlands Antilles, as well as numerous other regions. Dutch society changed with this increasing immigration. Inevitably, tensions arose between the established inhabitants and the new arrivals.

→ **Indonesia • Surinam and the Antilles • Diversity in the Netherlands**

14 The Netherlands in Europe

After World War II made way for the Cold War, the Netherlands became an advocate of Atlantic and European cooperation. Once the Cold War had ended, European cooperation rapidly gained momentum. In this phase, the Netherlands was also active in UN peacekeeping missions.

→ **Srebrenica • Europe**